Ink Dance:
Essays on the Writing Life

Ink Dance:
Essays on
the Writing Life

Deborah J. Ross

INK DANCE: ESSAYS ON THE WRITING LIFE

Copyright © 2014 by Deborah J. Ross
All Rights Reserved, including the right to reproduce this book or portions thereof in any form.

Foreword © 2013 Mary Rosenblum

Published by Book View Café 2015
P.O. Box 1624
Cedar Crest, NM 87008-1624
www.bookviewcafe.com

Print edition 2018
ISBN: 978-1-61138-757-5

Cover design by Dave Smeds and Maya Kaathryn Bohnhoff
Interior design by Marissa Doyle

Some of these essays have appeared in earlier versions on my blog, LiveJournal, and the Book View Café blog.

The scanning, uploading and distribution of this book via the Internet or via any other means without the permission of the publisher is illegal, and punishable by law. Please purchase only authorized electronic editions, and do not participate in or encourage the electronic piracy of copyrighted materials. Your support of the author's rights is appreciated.

In loving memory

Mary Rosenblum (1952-2018)

Beloved friend, colleague, teacher, dog-lover, aviator,
and writer extraordinaire

Contents

Foreword by Mary Rosenblum   1

Just You and a Blank Page

Getting Started in Writing   3
Negotiating with the Idea Fairy   6
Warm Ups   9
 Open Here   12
More on Story Beginnings   16
Structure, Shape, and Interest   18
Do You Outline Your Novel? Should You?   21
Dream a Little Dream   26
It's Only Fiction   29
Not Just Another Funny Forehead:
   Creating Alien Characters   32
Villains, Evil, and Otherness   35
Revenge and Retaliation   39
First Person Perils   42
Why Write Short?   45
Why Write Long?   49
Sexuality in Fiction   52
The Magic Notebook   56
Focus   59
Write It Again, Sam   62
More Thoughts on Revision   65
Critiquing vs. Editing   68
Strategies for Dealing with Writer's Block   71
Overcoming the Inertial Hump   74
Sam in Spades: Why Not to Revise   77

Career and Survival

Queries, Synopses, and Other Uneasy Friends, Part 1   81
Queries, Synopses, and Other Uneasy Friends, Part 2   84
The Pitch and Why I Should Care   88
Book Promotion Rehabilitation   92
Non-Obnoxious Book Promotion, Part 2   96
Gatekeeping in the World of Ebooks   100
Story and Self   105
Stages in a Writer's Development   108
Blackberry Writing   112
When a Story Isn't Ready, Part 2   116
Series as Career Killer   119
How Gossip Can Trash Your Writing Career   121
Reviews: the Good, the Bad, and the Ignorable   125
Surviving Dry Spells   129
The Magic Phone Call   132
Letting Go, Moving On   136

The Writer's Life

Where Do You Write?   143
Writing Without Electricity   146
Interruptions   149
When Writing Friends Aren't   153
Creative Jealousy   156
Encountering Wannabee Writers   159
The Lady (Actual and Honorary) Writers' Lunch   163
Mentoring   167
Exercise for the Older Writer   170
Listening   173
When Is It Enough?   175

Nourishing Yourself

Surviving as a Writer (or Artist…or Musician) 181
Defining Writing Success as Publishing 185
Would You Write Anyway? 188
Zen Yoga Writing Practice 191
Nothing Creative is Ever Wasted 194
'Tis the Season to Get Crazy 197
Pacing… 200
Community and Solitude 202
Cross Training for Writers 205
On Writing and Healing 208
Writing Fears 211
Goals vs. Wishes 214
Settling in Meditation and in Writing 217

FOREWORD

Deborah Ross introduced herself to me at the first Science Fiction conference I ever attended in Portland, way back in, hmmm…must have been 1989, right after I'd started selling my short stories and showing up in the reviews as a 'hot new writer.' The 'new' part was certainly true and I was so flattered when this established author introduced herself and had clearly heard of me. We've been good friends ever since, through the ups and downs of our personal lives and our careers. Deborah is one of the 'stayers' in the New York Legacy publishing universe. Like me, she was never a blockbuster best seller, but she worked with Marion Zimmer Bradley, a very big name in fantasy, to help Marion complete her works as her health failed, and wrote her own science fiction and fantasy at the same time. She was able to stay on with one of the last truly independent Legacy publishers as other Big Six authors were being shed with the midlist, and is still supporting herself there today.

Deborah is the nurturing sort, whether she's critiquing, editing a submission for one of the anthologies she publishes, or giving advice to an aspiring author at a local writers' workshop. She makes writing work, and she understands *how* to make it work. She's a good teacher.

This collection of essays guides you through the craft and career of writing with all the useful information of a shelf full of 'how to' books, but offered with the warm personal energy of a conversation across the kitchen table.

From her advice on how to actually get started, her craft and career tips, to her really excellent counsel on how to survive writing in real life and still nourish yourself and your spirit, this collection offers an in-depth look at what it means to be a writer. Every day. All the time.

While Deborah's career has been New York oriented, most of what she has to say works for today's author going the small press or Indie route as well. She speaks of the things that helped her succeed or got in her way with a refreshing personal honesty that invites us to examine our own behaviors. There's a lot here for any aspiring writer who takes his or her craft seriously. No matter what you write or how you publish.

Read it, learn, and enjoy! You'll come away nourished.

Mary Rosenblum

Just You and a Blank Page

Getting Started in Writing

Writing a story—let's say it's your first—has some fundamental differences with beginning any other creative endeavor. At least, that's been my experience. I've never assumed that because I've seen an oil painting, I should automatically know how to paint one, or because I've heard a symphony, I can just sit down and compose one of my own. Yet just about all of us carry the expectation that we already know how to write a story.

After all, we're taught to "write" in school, so by the time the idea of putting our own stories down on paper occurs to us, we've had years of practice, or so we have been led to believe. We've learned to put pencil to paper and end up with something resembling recognizable words. We've put down sentence after sentence on such stimulating topics as "What I Did For My Summer Vacation," not to mention book reports, history reports, science reports, essays on current events, and so forth.

We get exposed to visual art—painting, sculpture, graphic design and the like—music, and storytelling from an early age. Even if we are not fortunate enough to experience these in live forms, we get bombarded by their images in television, films, and the Internet. I suspect the difference between writing (prose narrative) and other art forms is that we also use the same motions for other purposes. Going out on a limb here, I propose that if we sculpted our grocery lists or scored them for full orchestra, we might approach chiseling marble statues or composing a concerto for bassoon and orchestra with the same expectations of facility that we do when embarking upon our first novel. We've also most likely read—or had read to us—many, many stories. We've turned in all those school papers. How hard can it be to write a story?

Once we've got that question engraved in our minds, we fall prey to a number of fallacies. One is that we ought to be able to write a story without learning how. If it's easy, then any semi-literate primate can do it. If we have difficulty, there must be something seriously wrong with us. Second, and more crippling, is that we compare our internal experience of attempting to write a story with the finished products we read. Or, worse yet, with our memory of those finished products. It's been pointed out that "derivative" or "copy-cat" fiction (as an example, all the riffs on *The Lord of the Rings*) feels flat and gray because we can consciously recall only a portion of what's in the original. The rest contributes to the vitality of the work, but doesn't stick in that part of our memory that allows us to reproduce what we read. So we try to create a story based on the fragmented, incomplete, and biased memory of a work that has been through the editorial and publishing process. This is a recipe for frustration and failure.

Instead, a more helpful approach might be to first acknowledge that we don't know exactly how to go about creating a written story. We need to learn some stuff, and we need to experiment and see what works and what doesn't. We need to find out how we write, as distinct from how anyone else writes. We also need to know what we want to achieve, which is a fancy way of clarifying what it is we love when we read stories by other people and what we love about our own story ideas. This leads us to another crucial concept, which is that effective storytelling is not the same thing as transcribing that amazing movie showing within our own skulls onto paper. It's evoking a similar (but not necessarily identical) experience in the mind of the reader. That's how we get to where we want to go.

Now we're ready to ask: what skills do I need? How do the writers I love do this? How will I know when I'm on track? We've become teachable, if only by our own experience. We're on our way.

INK DANCE

Notes

Negotiating with the Idea Fairy

Where do you get your ideas? According to a highly successful writer friend, the Idea Fairy leaves packets of them under our pillows. When I tell people this secret, it's usually received with smiles. What's not said, but what working writers all know, is that's only one step in an entire process.

First, you have to invite the Idea Fairy into your life. Leaving out a glass of milk and a plate of cookies won't do the trick in most cases. (You never know. That toy train story might lead to fame and fortune.) Creating a receptive state of mind includes recognizing those tentative sparks, even if you aren't prepared at that moment to give them the attention they require to grow into fully fledged plot outlines. People vary in what suffices: for some, it might be a simple "wow, that's cool" moment; for others, jotting down the thought or image on a paper napkin serves to reinforce the generation of ideas. Anything that says to your creative muse, "More, more!" will work.

"More"? Is this woman demented? Doesn't she know I already have a queue of stories screaming at me to be written? The last thing I need is more!

No, the last thing you need is *none*. If you train yourself to ignore story ideas, the Idea Fairy will sadly pack up shop and go find a more welcoming host.

Second, you have to find a way to accept the gifts of the Idea Fairy, even when you cannot immediately use them. Acknowledge, yes. Promise the moon, certainly. Create a treasure-house of ideas, great. How about setting aside time, not necessarily huge chunks of it, for daydreaming about those ideas? It's fine to have them appear in their packets under your pillow, but not so fine if you never give them a chance to grow. How will you know which ones will blossom into truly cool stories and which had better ferment a while longer? Besides, do you really want to spend all your time on stories you have already started (or are under contract and heavily outlined)? Unless you absolutely loathe coming up with new material, it's helpful to carve out some play time.

Eventually, even the most die-hard I-must-finish-what-I-write advocate will find the time or market for something new. This leads to a third essential skill: the discernment of what size packets the Idea Fairy has bestowed.

Beginning writers often can't recognize the difference between a novel-sized idea and a short-story-sized idea. That's fine; for most of us, judgment comes with experience. It's like sculpting wood. A dense hardwood can support an elaborate design, whereas balsa or pine is more suitable for simpler shapes. Sometimes an idea comes in such a compact, neat form that it begs to be a jewel-cut short story. Other times, it's a keyhole glimpse of an enormous, gorgeously complex world.

I've been wrong in both directions—having what I thought was a short story explode into a novel, or else finding that the idea I wanted to flesh out into a novel was far more suited to a shorter length. My current project, an epic fantasy called *The Seven-Petaled Shield*, began as a series of short stories. I had so much fun playing in that world, I wanted to spend more time in it. To do so, I had to expand the original landscape and lines of conflict, but that's another story.

With time and thought, most writers learn how to gauge the heft and strength of an idea. "I reckon that's about 5,000 words," "Nope, novelette," "Looks like a short-short," or "Sweet heaven, I've landed a trilogy!" Nothing creative is ever wasted. Stories mature in their own time.

I still make mistakes as stories take unexpected turns, both in what I need to include and in what must be cut. But the Idea Fairy and I have worked out a pretty good understanding. I never forget to say thank you. And the milk and cookies don't hurt, either.

DEBORAH J. ROSS

Notes

Warm Ups

Athletes, dancers, and musicians all know the importance of warming up before going all out in their particular activity. Raising body temperature and blood flow to muscles, tendons, and joints helps make them resilient, thereby reducing the risk of injury. Range of motion increases. In the case of hard physical exercise, the heart rate rises gradually from resting into the target range. Adrenaline and other hormones prepare both body and mind to work.

What about writing? Do writer warm up? Do writers *need* to warm up?

Yes and no. And maybe. Writing is and is not like running track or performing *Swan Lake* (either the musical score or the choreography!).

Some writers dive right into a day's work. They champ at the bit, ready to boot up the computer or insert a piece of paper into their typewriters. Words don't just flow, they gush like a creative geyser too long pent up.

Then there are the rest of us. We fiddle, we daddle. We surf the net. We answer emails. We wash the dog (don't laugh, that chore—post close-encounter with a skunk—delayed the writing of this essay). We do anything and everything except put our fannies in the chair and our fingers to pen or keyboard.

Octavia Butler used to say that when she had difficulty writing, she did something she really hated. A class in accounting. Scrubbing toilets. Getting teeth cleaned. (I don't remember what examples she gave, but you get the point.) Okay, you say to yourself, you have a choice. You can do X or you can write the next chapter. My sister, a visual artist, employs the same tactic. I know she's in a slump when her house is inhumanly clean.

I suggest less-overwhelming alternative tactics to ease us over the inertia barrier. These things convey the likelihood that no matter how blank our minds are at the present moment, they will not remain so. Here are some things that have worked for me:

- "Morning pages" from Julia Cameron's *The Artist's Way*. One or more pages of longhand scribble, content irrelevant. The point is to keep the hand moving, the words—however inane—coming.
- The "all I have to do" game. All I have to do is read the last page/paragraph/chapter. Okay, now all I have to do is add one sentence. Good. All I have to do is one paragraph. One page… (Although usually by then I'm over the "hump").
- Work on something non-fiction. A blog, an article, an essay. A letter to a distant relative. This is tricky because it can also be a diversion. So limit it in length or time spent.
- Enter in my writing journal what I hope to accomplish today and commit to recording how the day's session went.
- Read a critique I've written of someone else's work.
- Write a paragraph on a "secondary" work—something just for fun (fanfic works great for some people). Agree that once I've hit my serious-writing goal for the day, I get another fling at shameless wish-fulfillment self-indulgence.

INK DANCE

Notes

Open Here

Author and former literary agent Nathan Bransford lists five openings to think carefully about using. He specifically did not say you *cannot* create an effective beginning with them, only that they pose particular challenges. This is a good thing, because my reaction to "never" and "can't" is "I love a challenge! I'll show you!" Here's his list of "Beware Beginnings:"

1. A character waking up.
2. A character looking in a mirror.
3. Extended dialog with insufficient grounding.
4. Action with insufficient grounding.
5. Character does X and, by the way, they're dead. (I have never wanted to open a story this way, I suppose there's a macabre, gotcha, Twilight Zone appeal to it; it's really a stupid trick to play on the reader, and, as a reader, I would not give that author a second chance.)

The first two are variations of the "white room syndrome." A character wakes up in a white room (and looks in a mirror). The white room or the empty room represents the blankness of the writer's mind. So instead of staring at a blank computer screen or sheet of paper, we stare at an opening setting. The mirror also serves as a metaphor for the writer having no idea who this character is, where he is, or what he is doing.

Here's the thing: I think these are perfectly good ways to begin *a draft*. Some writers are obsessive about working out every scene before they put it into words. They agonize over every sentence as they create it. Their first drafts are marvels of planning and precision.

I'm not one of them.

For me, a blank screen is like a glass mountain. It's too hard and thick to push through and too slippery to climb. Putting almost any words on paper/screen is my key to unlock the hidden door. Almost always, I will discard those first few pages, that first scene. But I need to start *somewhere*, to overcome that inertia, to give me something to tear down. If I am willing to write an idiotic opening—character awakens in a white room with no memory of who she is until she looks into a mirror—and let the words come, let the character speak to me, let the scene unfold, then I will, by slow stages or amazing leaps, be led to something of value. The white room is an act of creative faith.

The next two openings involve content without context, the content being either people talking or people doing things. Often the "shoot the sheriff on the first page" openings fall into this category. Bullets whizz by, people shout, there's lots of frenzy but we can't figure out what's going on or why we should care. For all we know, the sheriff getting shot is a good thing. Because the writer has not presented what we need in order to care about—or even comprehend—this content, it is impoverished, if not devoid, of meaning.

For all their drawbacks, these two openings have a small advantage, which is that *something* is going on. The temptation then becomes thinking we can flesh out the setting (all too often with flashbacks that destroy whatever momentum we've flailed around establishing in the first place). Because these scenes have the semblance of substance, it then becomes harder to rip them out, although it is almost always just as necessary as it is to delete the white room or mirror scenes.

When I was a fairly new writer, I thought I had to open with frantic action in order to hook the reader. I turned in story after story that were classic examples of "Action With Insufficient Grounding." Finally, one of my writing buddies, undoubtedly frustrated by my inability to understand what the problem was, asked me to describe an action-packed opening of a book I liked. I'd recently read Barbara Hambly's *Dragonsbane*, so I mentioned that. At his suggestion, I then took a look at what was really in the book as opposed to what I remembered. Yep, there's action (an ambush) but it doesn't happen until about 10 pages into the story, at which point I knew and cared about the characters and their quest.

I mentioned above the temptation to try to solve the "with insufficient grounding" flaws by adding more contextual material. In my experience, that doesn't work. What does work is admitting that this is the wrong Point of Entry, and trying coming into the story either before or after that scene. Before sounds logical. Write the set-up, then the action, right? But it isn't always right. What we're seeking is the sweet spot of instability that launches the forward momentum of the story. In that sense, the white room false-start gives us more freedom; we're less apt to be welded to those particular words.

If any of those openings (except the last, the dead guy) get us putting words down, moving into the story, writing stuff we know doesn't work but leads us to stuff that does, then I say, *Go for it*. Don't be afraid to make mistakes in that first draft. Make it rough, flop around, throw up lots of chaff and dust. Turn it into a fermentation vat of ideas, images, characters, dialog, events and non-events. Then you can do the winnowing. You can rewrite the opening from the perspective of having seen the shape of the whole story. Looking back, you'll be in a better position to see what that opening requires, what is best moved later in the story, and what is unnecessary, distracting, or counterproductive. In other words, give yourself the space and freedom to experiment.

The only draft that matters is the one on your editor's desk.

Notes

More on Story Beginnings

My usual strategy is to start writing *somewhere* because otherwise I'll just dither and fuss and glare at that blank screen. I need to get some traction, some momentum. Half the time, I don't know what I'm doing until I get the words down. I used to think there was something horribly wrong with me as a writer because this would happen even when I had a detailed outline. The outline would tell me where I was going to end up, but not where I was starting. As the years and stories rolled by, that didn't change. What did change was my ability to cut and slash and clear away the deadwood and add the stuff I didn't know I needed when I set out. In other words, the words of one of my workshop buddies, I learned to revise enthusiastically.

After some time, I got better at revising by using "diagnostics," that is, tools and strategies to help me pinpoint the weaknesses and just plain errors of my story. I don't do well with checklists, so they were "right out," as the Brits say. However, I'm strongly visual, so flow charts and diagramming a Three-Act Structure, complete with Plot Points, turned out to be really useful.

The opening should be something that piques our interest, like a literary appetizer. Is this a salad of spring greens with tangy goat cheese and hazelnuts? A crab cake? Deep fried jalapenos? Creamy butternut soup with freshly-grated nutmeg? Roasted garlic and rounds of crusty bread? Bruschetta or buffalo wings?

Does it make you hungry for more? Are you eager to dive into the Entrée section of the menu? Then it's done the job. On the other hand, if it sits in your stomach like a rock (indigestible exposition) or leaves you queasy (confused, disoriented by too many unexplained and frenzied events), you might want to re-think your presentation.

Notes

Structure, Shape, and Interest

I've been beta-reading a manuscript by a local writer. It's a middle-school novel aimed at boys. The prose is for the most part okay, and there's some particularly strong dialog. *Yet*...and any of us who have critiqued manuscripts know that *yet*...the story wasn't working for me. I could point to a number of superficial elements, but something deeper kept nagging at me. I adopted one of my standard techniques, which was to pay attention to when I got bored. Alas, the moments that engaged my interest were all too short. And yet, the story wasn't inherently tedious. What was going on? Was it simply that I have never been a ten-year-old boy?

It wasn't until I read Bill Bryson's hilarious memoir, *The Life and Times of the Thunderbolt Kid*, that I had an inkling of what was going on. Bryson's book centers on growing up in Iowa in the 1950s; some of the material is Iowa-nostalgia, some is 50s-nostalgia, but what swamps them both is Boy Stuff. Boogers and worms and vacant-lot baseball and mail-order chemistry kits and B movie matinees and a thousand and one tricks played on friends, each more grossly disgusting than the one before. The things that grabbed me in the friend's novel were exactly these (for instance, two brothers figuring out how to have water balloon fights through mini-time portals, although why they didn't shove their baby sister through one just to see what would happen was never clear to me).

This is a long way of saying that a story should have congruence between its structure (three acts, plot, etc.), its shape (rising tension, climax, etc.) and a third element, interest (the cool stuff, the things that make the reader perk up). The scene in which the boys discover how to use the time portals to ambush each other lasted maybe half a manuscript page, yet that was where the money was for this reader. The rest was just a travelogue of the we're-still-in-Kansas sort.

In general, the more intense the drama, the slower the pace should be. This means drawing the moment out and digging deep. When I began writing, I thought that if the action was fast and furious, it shouldn't take up much manuscript space. Just the opposite is true. Passages in which nothing exciting happens merit terse summary. Agonizing do-or-die moments, "the fate of the world depends on your next move," have the emotional strength to carry blow-by-detailed-blow narrative. (Not necessarily long sentences—in fact, short sentences and paragraphs work well.)

To return to the story in question, what the author had done was to skim the stuff that made this story different from all other stories (and in all likelihood, would appeal to the target audience). This created a discrepancy between the tension-shape and the interest-shape of the story. If I were to diagram the two, they would peak at different places and at different heights. The result is that I as a reader was left frustrated by not getting to explore and live out the fiendishly inventive adventures of two brothers, so I wasn't particularly interested in what was at stake in the climax.

After I'd set the manuscript aside for cogitation, I picked up a recently-published alternative-history novel. The book began with strange and wonderful twists on real history, a heady mixture of actual unsolved mysteries, and plots between villainous aliens and people who were true villains in history. Oh, and William Shakespeare. Twist built upon twist until, about half-way through, the book devolved into a depressingly conventional action-adventure. I felt as if all the wonder had been sucked out of that world. I'd been hoodwinked, a victim of bait-and-switch. I became so disinterested, I almost set the book aside during the climax. The cool stuff was all window-dressing, scene-setting for a blow-'em-up battle that could as well have happened in Poughkeepsie.

Good fiction of any kind offers us congruence between interest and action, between what grabs our imagination and what grabs our adrenal glands. Great fiction integrates not only our imagination and our hormones but our hearts as well.

DEBORAH J. ROSS

Notes

Do You Outline Your Novel? Should You?

It cannot be repeated often enough that there is no single right way to write a novel (or to paint a landscape or design a house). All these artistic endeavors require certain elements (plot, characters, tension rising to a climax, or motif and variations, harmony, contrast, or foundation, walls, plumbing, etc.) They vary in the point in the creative process at which those crucial elements must be in place. Within those parameters, there's a great deal of flexibility that allows for individual differences. What matters is not when a writer nails down the turning points, but that they are present and in balance with the rest of the book when it lands on the editor's desk.

Many writers attempt their first novels by the "seat-of-the-pants" method: writing whatever pops into their heads. Sometimes they end up with dead ends (disguised as "writer's block") and don't finish the work. Other times, they do finish, only to discover (either through their own perceptions or feedback from others) that the book has significant problems. So they write another draft and go through the same process until either the story works or they become so frustrated they give up, or they refuse to accept further critiques and then self-publish.

There's nothing inherently wrong with such a spontaneous approach to the first draft. A good deal of the pleasure of writing is in discovery, in not knowing what will come next as the adventure unfolds. This is how children play. A finished novel usually requires a separate editorial, self-critical phase, at least for most of us. That's neither good nor bad, it's just part of the process. If you want to "pants" your first draft, you accept that you're going to have to revise. Maybe a little, maybe a lot. Some writers loathe revision. I happen to love it.

At some point, it occurs to many of us that if we maybe thought about what was going to happen in our novel and how we were going to portray it, that we might save ourselves a bit of revision time. We might even jot down a few notes, reminding ourselves that this is just a tentative sketch and that nothing is carved in granite. We may and most certainly do change our minds when we discover that the actual story has diverged significantly from our strategy. I've been known to rework my notes, negotiating the borderlands between spontaneous writing and ill-thought-out plan.

Some writers never go any farther with outlining. They decide it's not working for them, whereas it is actually not working, period. Outlines help because they are a place where problems with story elements can be worked out in a relatively short time and wordage. They reduce the number of dead ends, plot holes, and inconsistencies in motivation. But in order to realize the benefits of outlining (or planning, if you're allergic to the word *outline*), they require concentrated and creative problem-solving.

Outlining—proper, thoughtful outlining—is exhausting. For one thing, it's concentrated. A typical outline is five to ten single-spaced pages, maybe 2,000-5,000 words, summarizing a work that will be 100,000 words when completed. That's an immense amount of thought crammed into very few pages. For another thing, the actual writing of a story can generate its own positive-energy loops. You get excited by an idea that pops up, or a character takes on a life of her own and runs away with the story, or some lovely phrase or bit of dialog strikes you as so wonderful, it makes your heart sing. These moments are precious but rare in actual writing. I'd venture that they are non-existent in outlining.

So outlining can be energy-draining and tedious. Why then do some writers swear by it? For one thing, as I mentioned above, when done properly it saves time. For a new writer, struggling to learn the craft and working on spec, this may not seem like such a big advantage. For a writer trying to earn a living, it can make the difference between completing one book every three years and managing two or three per year. Most established writers who are able to sell "on proposal" have no choice. Editors (and agents) expect synopses (which are not exactly the same as outlines, but are interchangeable for the purposes of this discussion) and sample chapters.

Outlines, like pitches and queries, are also the occasion of dread in the minds of writers because they require a different skill set than actual story writing. Pitches and queries are marketing tools. Outlines are blueprints, not novels themselves. When I have to write one, I go around muttering, "If I could have told the story in ten pages, I wouldn't have had to write 500! Growl-growl-growl!" I have to patiently re-remind myself that I wasn't born knowing how to do this, that I do it infrequently enough to lose whatever facility I gain each time, and that I cannot do it quickly or casually. For every element I write down, I will most likely need to get up, pace, take the dog for a walk, mull it over in a bubble bath, and then come back with a deeper insight into what the story needs.

I think of composing the outline as layering the story, but with filo dough, not bricks and mortar. I start with whatever grabs me—an idea, a character, a situation, some bizarre twist of events, or sometimes even just an emotional tone. Then I play around with *Would it work this way? How can I jack up the risks? What terrible thing will result if this other thing does not happen? (And then that's what I put in, of course.)* I almost always realize that this won't work and that won't work, or I need another character to put sand in the gears, or the danger just isn't grave enough to justify all the hoopla.

This leads me to what may be the most valuable gift of careful outlining: it gives me a chance to set the stakes, to "build in" escalating drama, and to plan out how I'm going to parallel the hero's emotional journey with his outer adventures. In other words, to shape the overall dramatic story arc so I will know where I am and what needs to be going on at every stage. Some writers like to use terms like *plot point, midpoint empowerment, climax*, etc. I like to draw flow charts and diagrams. It doesn't matter what jargon describes the strategy; what's important is that I have one.

For all my enthusiasm for outlines, gained over three decades of exploring all the ways to do it wrong, I also appreciate the importance of spontaneous writing. I don't approach novels in this way, but I think my creative spirit would be the poorer if I did not have some way of following my own lighthearted inclinations through a story. This is one reason why I continue to write short fiction. For me, it provides a playground where I don't have to think about structure or rules, I can just flow with whatever wacky notions come to me. Daydreaming is like this, only even less structured. I know many professional authors who (still) write fanfic, and I suspect it fills much the same function. So in the end, the question of whether or not to outline is not either/or, but finding the balance between "pantsing" and "micro-managing" that keeps our inner children joyful and allows us to put forth our best work.

Notes

Dream a Little Dream

Dreams can offer us a wealth of startling images, bizarre encounters, and fantastical situations. At their most memorable, they convey the emotional texture of our deepest longings, our most paralyzing fears, the memories we would as soon forget but must not, and the people we will never see again, for good or ill. The stuff of great stories, right?

Wrong.

Well, maybe. The problem with using dreams as story material is the very illogic nature of them, the juxtaposition of images and actions without regard for the laws of physics, psychology, or anything else. Without delving into the analysis of dreams (neurological or Freudian), I can safely say that the same process that make some dreams so powerful also makes them highly personal. The dream-story that unfolded between your ears last night was your individual brain at play, uncaring of the waking conventions of shared experience and assumptions. Simply put, your dreaming mind is a world unto itself. No translator is available.

Throughout ancient times in many different cultures, prophets and sages attempted to interpret dreams, to create an overlay of sense. Often, this required a considerable feat of mental gymnastics. When in doubt, they could call it a prophecy and proclaim that all would be made clear. Eventually. We're still waiting on quite a few of those.

Yet dreams move us, terrify us, inspire us, and linger in our waking thoughts. As long as we respect their idiosyncratic nature, they can become a treasure trove of idea-seeds. With perspective, discernment, and literary craft, we can turn them into stories that will mean something to a reader, too. The trick is not to transcribe the dream but to *transform* it.

Jaydium, my first published novel, began with a dream-image: a tunnel, dark and poorly lit. A ghostly figure of a man floats there, his feet not touching the ground, his hands passing through the rock walls. In itself, this is not particularly innovative. I'd seen something like it many times in film. Usually, the figure is adrift in time or some cross-dimensional warp. The hero's goal is to rescue him, to bring him back into normal space/time.

As I started playing around with the image, I wondered what would happen if such an attempt might have the opposite effect—to bring the rescuer into wherever or whenever the adrift-guy was. Again, this was not terribly original, but had more "story-ness" that the starting image. Notice that what I did was to take a situation and ask, "What if?"

About a hundred rounds of "What if?" later, I knew I had something. My rescuer had become a pair of unlikely allies, each with a different reason for being in the tunnel, and I'd set up not one but a series of "getting knocked sideways," not only back in time but across alternate histories. On the way, my pair picked up more companions (including the ghost), outwitted some nasty pirates, and ended up in the clutches of an alien scientist. So far, so good. But not good enough.

I wanted something more at risk than just "not getting home." What if (those magic words) getting home meant something else happening, something really terrible that affects much more than just these few characters? What if the alternate future in which they don't get home was the best one?

At last, I had the makings of a story—four characters with different, not necessarily compatible goals, and a dilemma each of them must face. I have conflict between characters (and cultures) as well as within my primary characters, not to mention some spectacular scenery and a ticking doomsday clock.

Now we're cooking!

Notes

It's Only Fiction

At the best of times, I'm mildly schizophrenic about my story-telling. Actually, that's an inaccurate use of the psychiatric term. I mean, inconsistent and of two contradictory minds. On the one hand, I think it's essential, even life-saving, to tell the truth about who we are, how we feel, and what we have experienced. I'm struck over and over with how telling our personal stories has the power to transform not only our own lives, but those of the people around us. On the other hand, I also believe that good fiction operates on somewhat different principles than real-life one-event-after-another. It has a beginning, middle, and end that give it shape. I'm far from original in saying that good fiction is more true than life, not because it is more credible but because it requires an emotionally coherent story arc.

"Write What You Know" may be good advice in terms of emotional veracity, but useless and counterproductive when it comes to gigantic silver slugs with space-faring technology, magical systems based on music, or boarding schools for wizards. Such beings and such worlds come about as a marvelous alchemical blend of research and imagination.

Like other fiction writers, I work hard to create characters that aren't me and situations I've never experienced. As a result, I'm not alone in having some reviewer or even fellow writer (who should know better) assume that I've drawn heavily on autobiographical material for my characters. (This did happen to me, and I can assure you that Kithri from *Jaydium* is entirely made-up.)

Things can be emotionally true without being literally true. I can remember how it felt to be in such-and-such a situation or having done this-other thing. Like many (most, I daresay) writers, I love hearing other people's stories, and I am as guilty as the next person of taking mental notes about adventures and experiences that are different from my own. So although this-particular thing never happened to me, this is how I imagine it felt like, having listened to someone it did happen to. If I do my job as a writer well and bring a writer's sensibility to the problem, then I can end up with a story element that rings true.

The other side of this coin is what to do with my own life story. Keeping my experiences secret is one option (not a very healthy one, in my opinion), and telling them only in certain private settings is another. Putting them down as a memoir is yet another. Like lots of other people, I've had the impulse to turn mine into a work of fiction. Half the people I mention this to think it's a wonderful idea and the other half warn me not to even try. Most of the time, I am not at all sure it's a good idea. I suspect that the very things that were pivotal for me, the things that moved or shook or inspired or devastated me most, don't fit well into fiction. So I'd have to be willing to "kill my darlings," not just the prose bits but the sequence of events and in many cases, the events themselves. My fear is that in doing so, I will come perilously close to lying about what happened to me. It's often been a struggle to delve deep enough to discover my own truth, and I wonder if fictionalizing it will eviscerate its meaning for me. I still haven't come to a resolution about this and would welcome any thoughts.

There's another way to look at all this and that is to take those critical moments and to use them as kernels of fictional moments. I may bedeck them with completely different circumstances. I may make sure the characters involved in no way resemble those in real life. I may situate them in a plot arc having nothing to do with "what really happened." I may change all these things in the service of crafting a story. I may even change the pivotal moment itself but use its emotional energy as a driving force, a lens through which I focus the momentum of the story. So far, that's worked the best for me: passion and tears poured out on the page.

In the end, all stories are made up. All stories are true. They are, after all, only fiction.

Notes

Not Just Another Funny Forehead: Creating Alien Characters

All too often, television and films have depicted alien races as either shapeless blobs bent on wholesale destruction or else human actors with wrinkled noses or pointed ears. Alas, printed media have not proved immune to such generic and often salacious depictions. Fortunately, enough science fiction (and fantasy, if elves, talking dragons, and the like are "aliens") authors have either the scientific training or the resourcefulness and imagination to do careful research. Both genres abound in well-crafted, intelligent, nonhuman species. Much has been written on the topic of "how to design a really alien alien," and it is one of my favorite convention panel topics.

When I set out to create an alien race for *Jaydium*, however, I hadn't participated or listened to many discussions. At that time, aspiring writers were encouraged to use check lists in developing alien races and their cultures. I find check lists singularly unappealing! They remind me of a conversation I overheard while standing in line to register for my first convention: a person was holding forth (quite loudly and in excruciating detail) about a world he had created. My reaction was twofold: first, that I had never and could never design such an intricately-described place; second (which kept me from utter despair about my own writing) that there was no story there.

My aliens arose from my writing process. That is, I started with the forward momentum of the story, the characters under stress, the unstable setting, the cascading sequence of events that led inexorably to a climax. Only when I understood the demands of the story did I know what questions to ask. I realized fairly early in the writing process that the mineral jaydium was the result of the destruction of a wonderful civilization, a sort of cataclysmically-metamorphic rock with special properties. I wanted my characters to be faced with a choice of attempting to save that civilization (at the risk of there being no jaydium, and hence no way to get home) or to let the tragic events unfold. This led me to ponder, What kind of civilization? Created by what kind of beings?

Since I loved invertebrate zoology in college, I used the gastropod family as a model. In doing so, I violated a slew of biological realities (including the structural limits on size of creatures that don't have skeletons, internal or external, as well as the limiting rate of oxygen and carbon dioxide exchange). And yet, what I did worked. No one, not even my professor (to whom I presented a copy) railed at me for scientific idiocy.

Part of the reason, I believe, is that although my gastropoids were far from technically perfect, they formed an integral part of their world. I made them partly-understood, neither completely divorced from the reader's experience nor too-explained, too-familiar. I'd thought through how their secretions are used as building materials, their aquatic and dry-land functioning, their reproductive biology and its affect on their individual relationships, and their mode of communication.

However—and this is crucial—I didn't bash the reader over the head with everything I'd worked out. The gastropoids and their culture are experienced through the eyes of our human castaways, who of course are not going to be handed a textbook of alien physiology. As our viewpoint characters interacted with the gastropoids, I gave the reader enough information to understand what is going on, but not an overpowering, indigestible treatise.

Lessons: Respect your own creative process, whether organic or tightly planned. Respect your reader's intelligence and patience. Cut to the chase.

Notes

Villains, Evil, and Otherness

Writers and readers love bad guys. More often than not, they're more interesting—not to mention sexier—than the good guys. Of course they're attractive. They're dark, dangerous, edgy—in other words, forbidden fruit. Even Jane Austen's naughty boys have a certain intoxicating allure.

Bad guys are also more likely to be complex in interesting, tortured ways, and to be charismatic and cunning but with fatal flaws that prevent them from being heroes. They possess the capacity for grandeur, except for… But you know all this. You've read the rewrites of classics told from the point of view of the villain. You know every villain is a hero in his own story, it's just that his goals don't align with those of the protagonist, but none of them get up in the morning and say, "Evil! Evil! Rah-rah-rah!"

Why do we keep coming back to having villains, as distinct from flawed heroes or misunderstood monsters? Aha, you say, to provide conflict, to place obstacles between the hero and his goals. Sure, you say, because there are really only three plots: Man Against Nature, Man Against Man, and Man Against Himself. (I think this is an oversimplification, and I'm not at all sure it's true, but the point is that conflict *between* characters is one of the enduring themes in story-telling.) Once upon a time, all you had to do was put a man on a black horse or in a black hat, give him a mustache and a name with too many consonants, and everyone would understand that he had no redeeming qualities (and bad dentition). Later, it became desirable to give him a few aspects to admire and to play around with expectations. Then it became fashionable to portray him as not-really-bad, but wounded or misinformed or warped by his culture. Science fiction and fantasy, not to mention the whole of English literature, abounds in examples.

If we want a character (our hero, protagonist, viewpoint person) to struggle against something outside himself, we create an obstacle, a menace.

No matter how we clothe the obstacle-character in nifty-stuff, his or her function remains to make things difficult. The more dangerous, resourceful, and recalcitrant the obstacle is, the more dramatic the conflict. Who wants an obstacle that is sympathetic, compassionate, reasonable, or helpful? Courage and intelligence are fine, as long as they're in the wrong cause. But kindness? Loyalty? Humility?

We do the same things in our minds with our villains that we do with our real-world enemies. We selectively enhance those characteristics that make them less like us, less understandable. Less human. We transform them, we demonize them, and eventually we see them not as fellow men and women, but as "the other." We eliminate all possibility of an "I-Thou" relationship, substituting an "I-It" of the most pernicious kind. In many ways, I prefer Chthulu to human villains. It's absolute and terrifying and utterly incomprehensible. I wonder if the original vampires—not the sexy, sparkly ones—were so scary because they had the outward semblance of humanity, but their nature was antithetical to life. What's even scarier is when we start thinking about "those people over there" in the same way.

Then there is the problem of evil itself. Whether or not we begin with a belief in a universal force of corruption and harm-seeking, we will surely create it in our own imaginations by this process of turning an adversary into "the other." But aren't there people—and characters—who do terrible, terrible things? Aren't they evil? I think we use the word in different ways. If I said Hitler or Pol Pot or Stalin was evil, I would mean that they caused such horrendous suffering and committed such heinous crimes, that words fail me. It's shorthand for horror so great it will take generations to heal.

Evil in story-telling, on the other hand, can be a force in its own right, the distillation of everything that makes the hairs on your neck stand on end and your mouth turn dry, and the worst thing is that there is no reasoning with it, no way to bargain with it or earn its respect. None of the things that are important to us—integrity, generosity, fidelity, altruism, for example—avail against its implacable, relentless power. It will overcome and corrupt us no matter what we do. This is, I think, the shadow that has haunted Western civilization for a long, long time. If I picked any particular era, I'd have half my historian friends on my case, so let it rest as "a long time." My point is that it's influenced how we see those obstacle-characters, and how we distort the enemy-of-the-moment.

Regardless of our politics, as writers it behooves us to be mindful of how we portray our antagonists. I'm not suggesting that all quarrels can be resolved with a little touchy-feely therapy and a cup of tea. We want our protagonists to have something substantial and competent with which to strive, and we want the consequences of failure to be terrible indeed. But that doesn't mean we have to perpetuate hateful stereotypes. If you want your hero to wage a battle against Evil Incarnate, then make it a gloriously inhuman element. If you want your antagonist to be human, then make him or her gloriously human.

Notes

Revenge and Retaliation

Human beings have a tendency to lash out in retaliation. To take revenge for a wrong (whether actual or imagined), and to focus all resources toward that end. Such single-minded dedication makes for dramatic fiction. It is, after all, a form of self-sacrifice for a greater good—the righting of wrongs, the punishment of the wicked, the service of justice. It also presents a wealth of possibilities for action and for exaggerated emotion.

It's also a natural and, dare I say, universal human impulse. When someone hurts us, our first and automatic reaction is anger. I think this is true, no matter what our religious beliefs, our social conditioning, or our meditation practices. These things influence how we express our reaction, but I don't think they can eliminate it. We want to strike back. Anger can be immensely helpful in energizing us to life-preserving action. It also has the result of temporarily numbing both physical and emotional pain. In the natural course of events, however, this reaction is brief in duration. We humans—and the characters we create—run into problems when we become frozen at this stage. Then our brains start thinking, "I've got to make her pay," or "That'll teach him." Armed with righteous justification, we start planning out our revenge, distorting our lives to creating suffering in others.

In fiction as in life, actions have consequences. As writers, it behooves us to understand the difference between natural consequences and created or artificial consequences. If Character A is an habitual liar, the natural consequence is that anyone who's had dealings with him will become distrustful. People may also be angry and resentful if they've been harmed in other ways. A created consequence might be someone slaughtering A's favorite guinea pig and hanging the carcass outside A's door. The distinction here is not only one of appropriateness but of scope. Cheating at poker has natural consequences within the game (and its financial obligations); fire-bombing the cheater's home town escalates the conflict to an entirely new level.

This is useful to understand when we're looking at a character's motivation. It's all too easy to set up:

A harms B or someone/something B cares about
B dedicates himself to revenge
B sacrifices all other aspects of his life in pursuit of this goal
B achieves his aim
B lives happily ever after.

If we break it down to immediate/natural vs created reactions, we can add a few twists:

A harms B

B is hurt, furious, incredulous, desperate, despondent; other characters react to B's plight

B dedicates himself to revenge in a way that makes his reaction different from that of any other character because it's shaped by his own history, values, etc. This can be done coldly and with calculation, or unconsciously, or in a delusional way; B can be manipulated by those with other agendas and reasons for wanting A eliminated.

B sacrifices all other aspects of his life in pursuit of this goal, despite many possibilities of taking some other action. The conflict assumes a larger scale, with other characters being drawn into it or affected in powerful ways; perhaps B has moments of awareness of the price but is, like an addict, unable to change; perhaps B wrestles with his decision, thereby gaining inside into himself and A.

B achieves his aim or B changes his mind as a result of what he's suffered.

B comes to terms with the full impact of what he has done, for good or for ill.

I think that's a much more interesting story.

Notes

First Person Perils

Every writer I know has an opinion about point of view (POV) and a personal preference as well. It's rare to hear someone say she enjoys writing omniscient third every bit as much as first person. We've all got our quirks shaped by our personalities, our experiences as readers, and what books on writing we've read or teachers we've studied with or editors we've worked with.

Writers do not agree on POV. There is no "party line," no singular truth about "which is better." (See my first point.) The obvious explanation is that different POVs are better suited to different types of stories. The less obvious explanation is that POVs are subject to cycles of popularity. Today the publishing world values the 3 i's: *immediacy, intensity, and intimacy*. This hasn't always been so, and may not continue to be so. The Victorian writers embraced omniscient third, and saying that their work was therefore inferior is a bit like saying Baroque music isn't as good as Romantic because it has more ornamentation.

Here's my take on the issue. Far too many beginning writers fall in love with first person. It's popular, especially with best-selling genres (YA, paranormal romance, etc.), so chances are we've read it, alas in our formative years. First person gives *the illusion* of the three i's, whether it genuinely creates them or not. It's a trap that's especially deadly for beginners. All they see is that first allows them inside the head of the protagonist, so the reader gets to experience the character's emotions at a raw, gut level *that is not achievable any other way*. I think this is nonsense. (Actually, I was about to type a stronger word, one syllable, but got polite at the last instant.) If I find myself thinking I *have* to use first, that I *can't* use third, then I am in danger of being complacent and superficial.

First person carries with it a temptation to writerly arrogance. I might venture to suggest it *creates* writerly arrogance because of the splash and ease of angsty melodrama. We don't have to consider all the nuances of a character's behavior, movement, speech pacing, posture, vocal tone, word choice, what details he notices and which he ignores, not to mention those he doesn't see but which are important, in order to know what he's feeling. He tells us in so many words, and we get lazy.

Writing in first person is like walking a tightrope with blinders on. It's far, far harder to do well than it looks. There's so much we can't do, and so much we can and should do but don't because of this illusion of emotional accessibility. Well and appropriately done, it's a marvelous feat of skill and control. It's just too dratted easy to do poorly.

As writers we have an immense amount to learn from actors, not to mention screenplay writers. Because they tell a story only from the outside, they pay close attention to all the ways humans communicate. In many ways, third person, whether tight or distant, encourages us to incorporate these dimensions.

I'm as guilty as the next one of indulging in first person, thinking I was making the story more vivid and immediate. Through many missteps and some very sage feedback, I began to question my choice of POV. Rewriting in third was an eye-opener. It revealed all the places I'd skimmed over crucial material, all the lazy assumptions… in other words, sloppy writing hidden under overemotional first person POV. I set aside first person, with considerable respect for its power and seductiveness, and worked on craft issues. I do sometimes write in first person now, but only when it is the best way to tell the story, when the strengths of this POV are assets, not smokescreens for poor writing.

This may not be true for every writer. I certainly hope it isn't. I'm happy to admit that we each have our temperamental preferences, and perhaps I am leery of first person for reasons peculiar to myself. I'm even more suspicious of wedding myself to only one POV—first, tight third, flexible third, omniscient (I won't even discuss second; I've never been able to contemplate writing it.) One of the tasks of a beginning writer, as I see it, is developing as broad a range of skills as possible, as big and varied a tool chest. First person POV certainly belongs there, but if all you have is a hammer, everything looks like a nail. As glitzy as first person is these days, I think it should be handled with great care.

Notes

Why Write Short?

The facile answer is, "That's the length of the stories that the Idea Fairy leaves under my pillow." The question is a whole lot more complex than that, for both writers and readers.

The perennial conventional wisdom is that a new writer ought to learn to write short stories before tackling a novel. The theory goes that working on shorter lengths will allow you to master various aspects of prose and storytelling craft while giving you the satisfaction of actually completing a story in a reasonable amount of time. We all need those gold stars, right? the more so when we're struggling to learn something new.

Another argument for "short first, then novel" is that you can establish your professional chops by selling to magazines and anthologies, and thereby achieve the name recognition that will help get your novel read or represented. When your novel does come out, you'll have a reader base.

This strategy has certainly worked for many writers in the past, and undoubtedly will work for many more in the future. That's because most—*but not all*—writers are creatively-wired to work at different lengths. It was and still is easier for most—*but not all*—writers to sell a short story than a novel. Let me elaborate:

The theory of learning to construct stories by writing shorter lengths (if we extend the category to include novelette, up to 12,500 words or about 50 manuscript pages) presupposes that we can thereby focus on only a few elements at a time. There will be one major plot line and relatively few characters, and the setting will not require great elaboration. This is an overgeneralization, of course. Short stories don't often feature an array of subplots and cast of thousands (unless they're nameless hordes).

What's wrong with this argument is that short stories by their very nature are compact, as opposed to the expansiveness of a novel. Every detail, every element must do double or triple duty (for example, a line of dialog might reveal character, advance plot, and evoke the world or society or family relationships at the same time). While it requires concentration to juggle multiple subplots, it is not proportionately more difficult than depicting a single line of action. Characters still need to be well done; settings still need to be specific rather than generic; dialog still needs to have certain characteristics, etc. The difference is that you have to do all that in, say, 5,000 words instead of 100,000 words.

Another problem with the conventional wisdom is that the print market for short stories has shrunk dramatically in recent decades. *Dramatically* is too tame a word. Very few anthologies are being published nowadays compared to a decade or two ago, and of those, even fewer are open to unsolicited submissions. Instead of 20 or 30 paying magazine markets, we have a handful. So the new writer who thinks it's easier to sell a short story may be sadly mistaken when he finds himself in competition with multiple award-winning authors for the same few slots.

Perhaps the most powerful objection to the short-first-then-novel dictum is that one size does not fit all. Some writers are natural novelists and struggle painfully to learn to write at the same time as trying to master a length that doesn't make intuitive sense to them. Once they're seasoned professionals, most of them can write short if they have to, but without the ease of their preferred length. Other writers naturally think short; it's how their minds work, and I've always thought it a shame to waste that brilliance forcing it longer and longer until all the joy has been stretched out of the story.

The explosion in epublishing promises to bring some interesting changes to the field. Now we have magazines that are entirely online or downloadable, without any print versions at all, and others that offer both. Established authors can bring out not only their novel backlists but their out-of-print short fiction in electronic form. Original works at both lengths are widespread. Short fiction is especially attractive to people who prefer reading their stories on handheld devices; short stories are perfect for airports and waiting rooms, offering the satisfaction of being able to finish the story in a single sitting. The low prices of short stories add to their appeal. Being able to purchase and download stories individually allows the buyer to tailor-make her own anthologies. It's entirely possible that these developments in publishing technology will lead to a renaissance in short fiction as an art form. I hope so, but I wouldn't count on it to pay the rent. At least, not yet.

Harry Turtledove once said that novels teach you what to put in a story and short stories teach you what to take out. What's left, at its best, is a jewel whose every facet is precise and clean-edged, a thing of glory to read and wonder to write. A great short story packs a different kind of punch than does a great novel, and one does not substitute for another.

So why write short? For me, there's only one good reason (aside from being powerless over what the Idea Fairy leaves me). That's because I love the form. I love writing it, how it makes all the parts of my creative brain go into hyperdrive, that *zing!* when everything I've set up crystallizes, and the high wire act of having to get it exactly right. I love reading it because I'm in awe of a story that excels in doing so much in so few words.

Notes

Why Write Long?

Why slave over the completion of 100,000 words, a year-long project for many of us, when you could be done in a month's mere 5,000?

The obvious answer is that novels and short stories aren't interchangeable.

Most of the authors I know, myself including, have misjudged the "weight" of a story idea from time to time. Occasionally, I'll start work on a novel only to have it fizzle in a chapter or three when I realized I've already said everything there was to say, and in far too many words. That central-core idea simply wouldn't support chapter after chapter, no matter how many secondary characters, narrative descriptions, or turns-of-fortune I stuck in. Likewise, I've found myself in the middle of what I believed to be a short story, when it felt like someone exploded the walls of my house and I'm floating in the middle of a galaxy—the world got suddenly much, much bigger.

A novel isn't a short story that goes on longer. It took me a long time to learn this, and in the end, I needed someone to explain it in words of one syllable. Even "episodic" novels have an underlying (or maybe it's over-arching) structure that distinguish them from a series of short stories thrown together like pearls on a string. Decades ago, I tried to write a novel that way (the pearl-stringing way), beginning with a short story (published) and then a sequel to that story (also published). I loved every new adventure that I put my characters through. The problem was just that: each was a new adventure. Having the same characters and a loosely-woven ultimate quest did not weave these stories into a whole. Perhaps a more skillful writer could have done it, but not me. The result lacked what you might call "shape." It was a series of equal-sized humps, not a single mountain.

So why would I want to do that, anyway, besides the obvious dictum that career is spelled n-o-v-e-l? Once I had several true-novels (of publishable quality) under my belt, I came to appreciate what novels do so well: generosity. Generosity to the reader, but also to the writer. A novel is to a short story what a marriage is to a one-night stand, however glorious that might be. Novels offer us the space and time to savor, to return, to create interconnections, layer upon layer of them. The visit to Pemberley might be accomplished in a short story, but breakfast with the Bennett family, chatting about the Netherfield ball, listening to Mary's awful piano playing, and analyzing the letter from Mr. Collins… those are possible only in a novel.

The expansiveness of a novel is not a justification for an indigestible expository lump (writerspeak for "way too much information for its own sake presented all at once"). As in a short story, every part of a novel must do a job, but there is more time and space in which to work. If I've fallen in love with a character, a family, a world, I want to share my delight in their company. I want to explore Middle Earth a bit, sing with Tom Bombadil, walk the twilit paths of Lothlorien, and sit on a sunny bank in the Shire before I go storming off to Mt. Doom.

If I've done my work as a novelist, all those moments, all those nuances and subtle connections all come together in a seamless whole. The thrill of getting it right is one of the best there is.

Notes

Sexuality in Fiction

A few years ago, I had the privilege of editing a new fantasy anthology series, *Lace and Blade*, from Norilana Books. The concept was a certain flavor of elegant, romantic sword and sorcery, witty and stylized, sensual yet with plenty of swashbuckling action (think *The Scarlet Pimpernel* with magic). Because we wanted to release the first volume for Valentine's Day, I contacted a group of seasoned professional authors, people I could depend on to understand what I was looking for and to deliver top quality stories to deadline. For various reasons, the publisher insisted that the second volume be open to submissions. If I had any idea what I was getting myself into, I would have refused. Insulated in the world of competent fantasy writers and readers who are versed in the grandeur of everyone from J.R.R. Tolkien to Tanith Lee, I was ill-prepared for what mundanes think of when they hear "fantasy."

Needless to say, when I talk about sexuality or eroticism or sensuality or gender issues in fantasy, I do not mean pornography. It seems that for far too many people, sexuality is such an emotionally difficult subject that instead of facing it honestly, discussing it openly, they shroud it in prurience and embarrassment, or else turn it into something salacious or forbidden. Yet just about every human being over the age of puberty has had sexual feelings (notice my delicate use of qualifiers). So if sexuality in fantasy does not mean "your most lascivious and pornographic imaginings, regardless of whether you'd really like to do these things, because how would you know what you enjoy if you've never been permitted to experiment," what is the role of sexuality in fantasy? Does it even have one? Should we keep sex out of fantasy literature, restrict the love stories to a chaste kiss now and again, and keep the hero/ine's mind firmly fixed on nobler causes?

I believe that sex is such a powerful force in human lives that it is impossible to portray the full scope of emotions and motivations without it. People might not, for a whole panoply of reasons, act on their sexual desires, but they have them. They have them in wildly inappropriate situations, as well as those times and places that nurture genuine emotional intimacy. The feelings are ignored or fulfilled, misdirected or frustrated, overly indulged or denied utterly. Freud had a few things to say about what happens when such a basic drive does not find healthy expression, and although his theories were dead wrong on many counts, he was not mistaken about the fact that sex will not go away simply because society (aka The Authorities, secular or clerical) disapprove.

There are at least two ways in which considerations of sexuality are important to any story: character development and world-building.

What are the attitudes and practices regarding sexuality in this culture? Is it permissive, repressive, or a combination? Is marriage life-long or fixed-term? Monogamous, polygamous, polyandrous? Do different cultures in your world treat love, sexuality, and marriage in the same way? How are sexual fidelity and jealousy regarded? Is marriage a personal or a business relationship? Who determines what is acceptable in sexual behavior? Have norms changed over time and if so, why? What are the social, moral, or legal consequences of transgressions? How can these be fulfilled or avoided? Are there times, places, or partners for whom "anything goes"? How does the culture deal with such activities—conscious forgetting, ignoring, teasing, or do these experiences form a special, perhaps a blessed, bond?

Where does a specific character naturally fall within the norms of his/her culture? How does he deal with the conflict between desire (or abhorrence) and expectation? Are other options (secrecy, emigration to a more compatible culture, open defiance) possible for him or her? Not all characters experience the same degree of sexual energy, and most will vary in their interest, depending on circumstances. Some will react to stress by becoming more sexual, while others will respond with diminished desire, even becoming asexual. Some interpret every personal interaction in sexual terms, and others are extremely private or compartmentalized. Interesting characters, like interesting cultures, are not monolithic in their sexuality.

Sexuality has a special role in fantasy stories because of its universality in human experience and its power. It's fairly common to use sexual energy as the basis for magic, but it's all too easy for a writer to fall into stereotypes. In some systems, magicians create power by channeling the sexual energy either of themselves or of someone else, making sex a necessary part of magical use.

But in other systems, sexual energy and magic are incompatible, leading to painful choices for characters and societies. This is the "virgin priest/ess" model of magical use, with the rather tired strategy of separating a witch/wizard from said magical powers by the expedient of rape. One of the problems with this model is that it takes most people considerable trial-and-error experimentation to figure out what works for them sexually, so I'm always puzzled how an inexperienced person is supposed to channel unfamiliar energies. More importantly, rape is not about sexual desire, it's about violence and violation. Sexual potency resides in the mind, not in the hymen. So if your world calls for a cult of virginal priests, it's better to come up with a more original scheme for relating lack of sexual expression to generation of magical power.

Notes

The Magic Notebook

No, it's not the title of my next novel. It's one of my most important writing tools. Maybe it will become yours, too.

I began keeping a writing journal after I'd made a few short story sales. Beginning in high school, I had been a fanatical diarist, not just to record the daily events of my life (how boring!) but as a file of story ideas, letters (all copied out), attempts at poetry and the like.

Once I was attempting to write fiction, my journals turned into magnets for other material: quotations, membership lists and schedules for my critique group, contact information for people met at conventions. But none of this proved as important as learning how to problem-solve on paper. When I began writing professionally, I never outlined or planned my stories. I wrote whatever came into my head. If something didn't work or the story had no shape, I had no diagnostic tools to show me what went wrong (let alone how to fix it). I used my journal for the intermediate step of turning ideas into a sequence of scenes. In order to make this different from an outline (I was adamantly opposed to outlines for many years), I used flow charts and colored diagrams. I made charts of characters and graphs of rising and falling tension, marking scenes with arrows until the graphs looked like pincushions. I wrote out character sketches. I never drew portraits of my characters (although I know some writers who do) but I stuck in lots of maps and floor diagrams.

Nowadays, it's easy to download software to keep track of characters, work out plots, etc. I've never used any of it. Why? Because when I write longhand, whether in a blank journal or a spiral-bound notebook, I use my brain in a different way than when I interact with a computer. In order to solve a problem like a plot idiocy or a character that won't cooperate or a total lack of inspiration regarding how our heroine is going to escape her doom, I want to come at it from as fresh and different an angle as I can. For me, that means changing media. I used to have a non-writer physicist friend who was a great sounding board for science fictional problems. Just articulating the problem, boiling it down to its essentials for someone who knew nothing of the story, helped me to distill what wasn't working.

The notebook serves the same function, which is a way of talking my way through a problem. Let's see, we have to get from here to there; what can go wrong? Make a list of catastrophes, no matter how far-fetched or idiotic (I use this technique for titles, too). Throw them all out. Make another list. Make a list of "If this happens, then that must surely follow." Write out each character's reaction to the worst of these. By this time, ideas are hopping like fleas all over my imagination. And I have a record of all my flailing-about: manure is wonderful fertilizer.

This leads me to the newest gift of the journal. That is, preparation for a day's work and reflection on how it went. It never occurred to me in the early years that I might need to get ready to write. I just did it! (And, conversely, if I was too tired, upset, etc., I wouldn't.) Part of writerly self-care is knowing how to move from "my brain is dead" to "my brain is alive." Part of professionalism is knowing what you want to accomplish and how you will do it—just for this day. It's important, especially when working on a long project like a novel, to set small goals and celebrate daily successes.

Even more profoundly, thinking about how I want to work and what I want to accomplish, and then writing down how it went, has generated a new way of evaluating each writing session. I used to set page quotas, as if they were the measure of creative output. (I still do, but softly.) Now I prefer to think of my goal as "working well." A single paragraph that is spot right on, that works on many levels, can be far more valuable than pages of unfocused wordage.

That's only the most recent way I've learned to use The Magic Notebook. I can hardly wait to see what else lies in store!

Notes

Focus

Some writers like a lot of structure. They make outlines, diagrams, and write out "beats" and plot points on 3 x 5 cards. I know one writer who writes out *scenes* on those cards. They have the "elevator pitch" down pat before they begin Chapter One. Then there are writers who, as I sometimes put it, "take a flying leap off the edge of reality" with no thought as to where it will take them. Often they're highly intuitive artists; their creative subconscious minds know exactly what they're doing, and the challenge is to get their analytical and critical minds out of the way so the story can flow.

I began writing like that. What was to plan? You got an idea, you sat down and began the story... and sometimes wrote yourself into corners, sometimes got muddled and bollixed and mired in the middle. Sometimes the end didn't fit, but all of this was okay because you fixed it in revision. I learned to revise. Extensively. Repeatedly. And Very Well.

With time, I started seeing those pitfalls/mine-traps/swamplands in advance, and I found ways to sketch out my way through them. I started thinking more about the whole story before I began writing it. I still don't like to over-plan. For me, a good deal of the fun of writing is exploring as I go along. I think it doesn't matter whether you outline in excruciating detail or discover the shape of the story after you've got a draft on paper. What matters is that at some point, intuitively or editorially, the necessary elements are all in place.

Which brings me to the idea of focus. Stories work because they have a central driving force (a motor, if you will). It can be a series of events, one catapulting the reader into the next. It can be the obsession of the protagonist. It can be a mystery, a puzzle, a scheme. Whatever. It's the organizing principle. One of the weaknesses of the seat-of-the-pants style of rough drafting, at least as practiced by me, is that I'm like a jackdaw in a costume jewelry store. *Oooh, a shiny! Another shiny! No, I like this other shiny better!* At some point, I need to pick or discern The Shiny Of All Shinies for this particular story.

That's where all those analytical pre-planning techniques can be helpful. I may not want to do all that stuff before I write the first sentence, but I can make use of them in other ways. They make wonderful diagnostic tools. *"Why is this story not working?"* So I take out the doctor bag, I shuffle through its contents, I try out different techniques—applying them *in retrospect* instead of *in advance*. And inevitably, I get exactly the insight I need to understand where the weakness is and how to take a new look at what I've got and how I can turn that into a strength.

I find it quite liberating that the words I've put down are not immutable. It was much harder to revise stuff when it was written in cuneiform on clay tablets that then were baked, or engraved in granite. Or even typed out, which is how I started. A story is a living, organic thing. You can give it a hard skeleton (internal or external) as it grows; you can let it germinate within a pre-created armature; you can allow it to toughen and solidify when it's at the appropriate maturation phase. There's no single way that's right for every writer and every story. What matters is that the final version, the one on the editor's desk, is crisp and vibrant.

Focused.

Notes

Write it Again, Sam

Last week, I finished the rough draft of a novel and after taking a couple of days to play, I have begun a second draft and am thinking about the process.

This second go-round has several important functions. One is to prune the most obvious infelicities, the repetitions, loose ends, and things-that-don't-make-sense. Of course, it would be better if I were thoughtful and accurate to begin with, but I've finally accepted that the first splurt of words on paper is always going to have dross with the gold. This will take me more than one go-round, so I need to get started.

The second is to get re-acquainted with the story. This particular book has been well over a year in the writing, partly because I was interrupted by editorial revisions and then proofing pages for a different project. When I resumed work, I did a pass through an earlier section to get back up to speed. The middle and final sections, however, have not, as it were, seen the light of critical day. This is an essential step before "re-vision." That is, in order to see where the overall manuscript needs re-shaping, re-writing, re-arrangement, I need to know what I have, to see the work as a whole. Otherwise, I'll just be cutting and pasting and shoving thing about without knowing what I want to achieve.

I've given up envying writers who are done with a work in a draft or two. I used to think there was something wrong with me because I couldn't do it. My first drafts were and still are drek. (I'm not being modest—I mean really awful.) Over time and with practice, however, I've come to appreciate that my own writing process isn't less than, it's just different. Fortunately, I like revisions. I give myself permission to do lots of them. That way, it doesn't matter how terrible that first draft is; what matters is what I do with it. Hence, mapping out the territory.

Along the way, as I have also learned, I will find gems of detail and nuance or moments of grace that I had no idea were there. Part of my job in revision is to make sure they don't get lost, by giving them the space they need, even if it's just tweaking the paragraphs. Small moments need quietness, even in the midst of frenzied action. So I'm on a treasure hunt as well.

It's not only permissible but important to savor what I've written. The gems make that easier, but even when faced with a chapter best expunged and rewritten from scratch, I allow myself to feel a sense of accomplishment. If a long time has gone by since I wrote these pages, I allow myself to feel surprised, even delighted. The next step—the execution of the massive slash and burn—is going to be brutal enough. I find it best to start with my confidence batteries fully charged.

Notes

More Thoughts on Revision

I've come across a couple of examples lately of authors reissuing books with significant changes from the initial publication or changing it relatively late in the initial publication process. With the rise of ebooks, the potential for rolling revisions to books is a very real possibility.

I've seen a number of instances of revising books after publication, and I often wonder how many are akin to the endless rewrites that beginning writers inflict on their maiden projects. It's easy in today's self-publishing climate to push a book to market before it's ready (or even if it is flawed enough to never reach the professional-publication threshold). Even if the original version went through the traditional editorial process, it may fail to meet the author's expectations and vision. Some years later, it's tempting to want to go back, armed with whatever improvement in skills and critical ability that have taken place in the interim.

Obviously, each case has its own circumstances, but most of the time, I think this is a mistake. It's not necessarily wrong in terms of improving a work that wasn't quite "ready," but it does place the author in a backward-facing position instead of moving forward to his or her cutting edge.

Revision According To Deborah:

1. *Change is Good*: I find it quite liberating that the words I've put down are not immutable. A story is a living, organic thing.

2. *Change is Necessary, So Start Rough*: I'm a writer who loves to revise, so I push myself to draft quickly and I don't demand that it be perfect. I start with a concept—a character, a conceit, an image, a mystery, a sequence of events, an emotional tone. As I draft, I labor under the delusion that this is

what the story "is about." More often than not, I'm wrong. I'm wrong because I'm going for the glitz, the superficial attraction. The truth is, I'm a better writer when I listen to what's underneath the glitz. That's where the emotional juice is, the deeper resonance, the Deborah vision.

3. *What Doesn't Work Is Your Friend*: characters that refuse to follow the pre arranged script, story elements that just won't come together, plot idiocies that are not just holes but dead end canyons—how can this be good? I've learned to rip all that stuff out (leaving chunks of bleeding, burning manuscript strewn about) and dig deep into the core. That's part of my revision (re vision) process, and although with time (read: decades of practice), I've gotten better at writing first drafts that are less superficial and more true, I still value this process. Throw away the chaff; be ruthless; seek the nuggets of treasure and bring them into the light.

4. *Cuneiform Has Its Place*: I love the way computers have taken the mindless re-typing drudge out of revision. However, word processors can be treacherous, particularly if I'm using a beautiful font. The words on the screen then assume the authority of print and impose an additional barrier between me and all the stuff that has to go.

Notes

Critiquing vs. Editing

Critiquing and editing are useful tools for making a story the best it can be, but they aren't the same thing. Both involve handing your precious manuscript, child of your dreams and the darling of your creative muse, to another person and asking what they think of it. In other words, even as we cringe inwardly at the prospect, we have granted them permission to say things we aren't going to like. Of course, we want to hear how much they loved it and all the things we did brilliantly. The point of the exercise, though, is to improve the story.

The most useful things I find in critiques are reader reactions, comments like, "I'm confused," or "This doesn't make sense," or "I don't believe this character would act this way." Or, simply, "Huh? You've got to be kidding!" Snarkiness aside, such comments tell me where there is a problem. The reader may be right about what the problem is, or what they object to may be the tip of an iceberg and the true problem lies elsewhere.

In critique format, I really, really don't want to be told how to fix those problems, and I don't know any writers who do.

At this stage, we're likely to be still in the throes of figuring out what the story is about—not our first preconceptions but the underneath, true, deep story. While it's invaluable to hear where we've gone off the tracks, we are the only ones who can find the tracks we need to be on. More times than not, those helpful comments come from the critiquer re-writing the story in her or his own imagination. That's natural because it's not fully formed yet, but no less un-useful.

Editorial feedback comes at a different stage of creation. We've found those tracks, and the story feels like it's come into its own. (Of course, we could be Way Off Base, but there's still a sense of integrity to the story at this point.) Now there is a thing to become more itself. That's been my experience of working with a good editor—she or he has the ability to look into the heart of what I'm trying to do, what the story is trying to be, and to see what would make it more so. So that's one major thing—the story's in a different stage.

The second difference is that—ideally—I'm now working as a team with my editor. This does not mean she gets to re-write or re-envision my book. It does mean that she brings expertise to the discussion. I am under no obligation to accept her suggestions of how to change the story. But I'd be throwing away an immensely helpful viewpoint if I didn't give those suggestions proper consideration. In my own experience, my editors have been right on in most of this type of feedback, and in those instances in which I objected strongly, I found the discussion led to even better ideas. Regardless, these are issues it behooves me to take seriously, whether I follow my editor's suggestions or come up with my own solutions.

I value both critiquers and editors; I think each brings something important to the maturation of a story. It's just not the same thing, at least for me.

DEBORAH J. ROSS

Notes

Strategies for Dealing with Writer's Block

One of the ways I pace myself in my writing day is to pace. I get up, move around the house, make a desultory attempt at some housework, take the dog around the block. If I'm really worked up about how a story isn't coming together or I've written myself into the black hole of all black holes, then I may dive into a cleaning project with a vengeance. Part of what's going on is I'm so frustrated, I need a constructive outlet for all that energy. I suspect that most of the time, I simply need some corner of the universe where I actually can create order, since the Work In Progress has temporary abdicated that role.

As it usually happens, just when I've got my sleeves rolled up, literally or metaphorically, the creative logjam un-jams itself and then I'm presented with a dilemma—do I drop what I'm doing and rush off to the computer (or at least a notepad and pen)? Or do I finish the d@#$%^ed task while I have some momentum? There's no right answer. I do different things at different times. Most of the time, I can't tell if the idea that hits me is The Exactly Right Idea or if it's only an opening sally and if I stay with what I'm doing (vacuuming, scrubbing bathrooms, sweeping the endless piles of oak leaves and acorns, weeding the garden, whatever) that More Will Be Revealed.

I used to believe quite fervently that there were such things as The Exactly Right Idea or The Ultimate Best Piece of Prose. I don't anymore. I've had too many instances where I haven't written down that idea or have lost that piece of writing (usually through my own idiocy in not backing things up properly/promptly, but from other causes as well), raged and stormed and grieved, and then came up with something even better. Whatever it was to begin with was only a draft, a preliminary to the main event. So in that sense, it doesn't matter what I do when I feel stuck and how long I do it for. The important thing is that it be an activity that gets my mind working in a different way, preferably one that does not demand all my mental faculties. Working on taxes won't do it, but washing dishes will.

This reminds me of how I used to write when my children were small. I'd use scraps of time, odds and ends, like the dishwashing I mentioned above, or the brief time before I fell asleep, to "pre-write" the next scene so that it would be so vivid in my mind that when I actually got 10 or 15 minutes to sit down at the typewriter (this was before I had a computer), I'd be primed to write like mad. I used to joke that I couldn't afford writer's block, I had so little time. Now I understand that I was using this same "un-sticking" technique before I was actually stuck.

INK DANCE

Notes

Overcoming the Inertial Hump

It often seems to me that we writers walk a high wire tightrope. On the one hand, the world is filled with excuses to not write, with diversions and distractions. The would-be writer who does nothing beyond researching his novel and never writes a word is an object lesson here. Life is full of things that "need" our attention. On the other hand, we're told over and over, directly and indirectly, that professional writers sit down and write. They put in their page or word quotas, come rain or shine. I've read how-to books that contain specific instructions on how to "train" yourself to write at the same time every day, no matter what else is going on or how you feel.

Sometimes I feel like a ping-pong ball, bouncing between two "shoulds." I should attend to my inner muse, let her lead me, write only when I'm inspired. Or I should approach my writing day in a professional and craftsmanlike manner, applying fanny to chair at precisely 9 am and immediately pouring forth the next scene. The fact is, neither of these strategies works for me.

It took me years to realize that I don't have to worry about being unproductive. I start beating myself up the moment I'm working at less than full-out crash-burn capacity. That's not everyone, that's just me. Maybe it's you, too. So the challenge then becomes, how do I find "cruising speed," a pace I can sustain, one that allows me to come up with new ideas, to ferment and cogitate and mull things around, not to mention have a life outside of writing?

The second thing I realized about my own working style is that almost always, once I get started, I'm fine. I regularly achieve my word or page goals, or if I do not, I've accomplished at least that much in creative or structural work. (For example, finding a misstep, taking apart the last couple of chapters and putting them back together so they work, might not add any pages but definitely is a good and productive thing!)

Sometimes, it takes me a while to apply fanny to chair. I call this process "settling." The reminds me that preparing to write is as important as the writing itself. More often than not, the reason I'm not ready is that my "back brain" is chewing over some point, either in the work to come or the work I've just done. Something's not quite right or I don't see the next step clearly. Words and images aren't popping into my mind. So I go off, play a Chopin Prelude, scrub bathrooms, balance my checkbook, walk the dog, sew on a button… and at some point, I'll either know exactly how to proceed or I'll be sitting down with the Magic Notebook; either way, I'm ready to work… almost.

The "almost" is the inertial hump, that final action of sitting down, email server and Internet browser closed, fingers on keyboard. This is yet another opportunity for me to castigate myself with accusations that range from laziness to incompetency. But it's just a hump. It's like those times when I want to call someone and the phone suddenly weighs 250 lbs and I pick it up and call anyway. I want to be anywhere but sitting at my desk, but it's an idle want. My real want, my true desire, is to get past it into the joyful state of writing. So instead of being an occasion of self-flagellation, I try to look at the hump as a funny little quirk of mine. It's annoying, true, but it has no power over me unless I grant it.

It's just a hump.

Come on, hump. Let's get to work.

Notes

Sam in Spades: Why Not to Revise

Creating a novel is more than putting text on a page, fleshing out characters, and polishing dialog. It involves the scope and soundness of the original conception. The process of turning an idea into a book has been compared to sculpting in wood. You take a block of lumber and you assess its density and strength, the fineness of its grain, its ability to withstand torsional stresses. If you're starting out with a soft wood like balsa or pine, it won't support a lot of elaborate ornamentation—you'd be better off with a short story. For a novel that involves complex world-building and multiple point-of-view characters, nuance and interwoven themes, teak or mahogany or even oak is required to "bear the weight."

Most of us begin our writing careers with pine-weight, plywood story concepts. If we keep reworking those stories, we prevent ourselves from going forward with what we have learned and developing denser, bigger stories. It takes an act of will, not to mention considerable intellectual courage, to just leave a story alone, to let it be what it is, and to begin again. Occasionally, we'll get cherrywood or stronger, but we're not skillful enough to execute a story that achieves its potential. In this case, when looking back and wincing and being unable to abandon the unrealized heart of the story, I think it's better to do a complete rewrite. Chuck the old manuscript or rip out everything that fails to measure up to the best you can do right now.

Begin again, with a true re-visioning.

Notes

Career and Survival

Queries, Synopses, and Other Uneasy Friends, Part 1

What do all these have in common? They are marketing tools that require you, the author, to in some way summarize "what your book is about" (and why the editor or agent should love it as much as you do). For most of my writing career, I have answered that question with an agonized cry: "If I could have told you that in a single paragraph, I wouldn't have had to write 100,000 words!"

Like many authors, I'm not terribly good at summarizing the emotional heart of my stories. I have all kinds of excuses: each reader's journey through the landscape of the story is different; the themes and subtext are evoked rather than explicit; it would take too long to detail the nuances and twists of the plot; yadda yadda, yadda. These are all excuses for a hard reality: the purpose of the query, etc., is *not* to duplicate the experience of reading the book. It is to arouse the editor's or agent's interest. By analogy, the purpose of cover art is not, as I once believed, to illustrate the story. It is to invite the reader to pick up the book. "Read me and you'll have this kind of experience," the painting says. As a reader, I'm annoyed when the artist has gotten the details wrong—the hero's eye color, the wingspan of the dragon, that sort of thing. Annoyed, but not betrayed. Betrayed is when the cover suggests a magical faerie realm and instead I find gritty military shoot'em-up space adventure, or get a steamy vampire romance instead of the anticipated witty and mannered steampunk.

It took me a long time to also understand that a query or synopsis is not what *happens* in the book but what the book is *about*. I had to have this explained to me very simply: in *The Wizard of Oz*, a dog runs across a prairie, an old woman catches the dog and puts it in her bicycle basket, a young girl talks with the farm hands, her aunt and uncle discuss local animal control regulations with the old woman. I've probably got the order wrong, but hope you can see that none of this conveys Dorothy's longing to find a place where "troubles melt like lemon drops."

I have learned two truths about writing queries and preparing pitch statements (even more condensed than queries!):

1. The skills necessary are not those I've used to write prose stories. I have to tell not show, to summarize and distill instead of portray. It feels as if I not only have to switch gears, I have to do everything backwards and inside-out. It makes my brain hurt. I have to remember that just as writing a technical manual for a space station is different from writing a Shakespearean sonnet, this is not the same as writing a story. I have far less experience in it. I should not expect it to be easy.

2. If I do my work carefully in composing a query, etc., the result can teach me valuable lessons about my own creative process. Although I outline some projects, I'm a fairly organic writer. Even when I have a pretty good idea where I'm going and where the plot landmarks are, I'm always surprised (sometimes delighted, sometimes horrified) by all the unexpected detours and discoveries. I joke that whatever I think a book is about before I start writing it, I'm wrong. The deep story emerges as I go, sometimes not fully until I've been through a revision (re-vision) or two. This isn't a problem, as I'm comfortable with both uncertainty and radical change.

Writing a synopsis in mid-process, for example, after the first draft, can be invaluable in helping me to see past the misdirections, the infelicities, the gigantic plot holes and character lapses. What's the heart, the core of the story—what's emerging like the giants from Michelangelo's blocks of marble? If I am willing to switch gears, no matter how uncomfortable that is, the result can be not only a richer, truer story but an immense savings of time. A five or ten page synopsis can eliminate a complete new draft.

Notes

Queries, Synopses, and Other Uneasy Friends, Part 2

What is a query and why should I learn to write one? The short answer is that once upon a time, you didn't need to. You could just send your completed novel manuscript to the agent or editor of your dreams, with or without a cover letter. You could be reasonably confident that either that person or some overworked assistant would actually read it. True, the turnaround time might be suspiciously short and the form rejection letter clearly one-size-fits-all.

These days, the number of publishing houses that read "unsolicited" or "unagented" submissions has shrunk alarmingly. The result is that editors want to maximize the chances of a manuscript being what they want before they invest the time in reading it. Most of the publishers who will consider work submitted "over the transom" have very long response times. Regardless of whether this is fair or even good business practice, it is widespread. Hence, marketing one's work means getting past a series of gate-keepers.

A query basically says, "Would you look at my book?" It does not say, "I'm a fabulous writer, so please shower me with money." It does say, politely and succinctly, "I've written a book. This is what it's about. Would you like to see it?" That way, the agent or editor can say, "Sure," "Sorry, we don't publish this type of book," "Sorry, we're overstocked," etc. A query should be short, a page or two at most, something an editor can read quickly. It should be as well written as possible because you have so little space in which to arouse the editor's interest. It should also be direct, not manipulative or cutesy. There are various opinions on whether to include biographical information or publication credits, but in general, it's best to include only the most relevant data such as experience directly related to the project or previous publications and awards in the same genre.

The "Sure" response is usually accompanied by submission requirements. "Send us a partial" or "the complete manuscript." Whatever the response, a wise writer follows these instructions. If an agent wants to see a synopsis and 100 pages electronically in rtf format, do not send a paper printout of the whole book. Chances are, it will generate a form rejection and a distinct prejudice against any further queries. "No thanks" can mean anything from the agent had a bad day and it just didn't strike her fancy to the letter was so badly-written the story stands no chance, to no publisher is buying cross-dressing teenage werewolf stories.

This is where a synopsis comes in. The agent has said he's interested, but he doesn't want to wade through the whole thing. He wants a good idea of the essence of the book and he wants to see a bit of the writing itself. He wants to know how you envision this book and if you can carry it off. Sometimes agents or editors will ask for one to three chapters, sometimes a given number of pages, for example, 100.

A synopsis is not an outline. Although it may describe the plot, it is not a blow-by-blow description of events. It's a way of communicating the *emotional* experience a reader can expect from the book. Usually it takes about eight to ten single-spaced pages to accomplish this, but requirements vary. A synopsis conveys not only the tenor and shape of the story, but basic information: Does it have a beginning, middle, and end? An identifiable climax? Does it fit within an established genre or is it daring and experimental? More importantly: Does the writer know what he's doing? Is this a book I can sell?

If marketing a manuscript is like arranging a marriage, the query is the listing in the dating service and the synopsis is the first date. You're trying to get a sense of the other person. You've signed up for an evening together, a little chat, a little dancing, maybe a nice dinner, but definitely not a lifetime commitment.

I'm not going to tell you how to write a synopsis. I've seen how-to instructions online and if I tried to follow them, I'd go nuts in five minutes. They make as much sense to me as a checklist for writing a novel does. I think it's as important to convey your distinctive voice in a synopsis as in the text of the story itself, which means not sounding like a pale copy of anyone else. When I sit down to write a synopsis, I pretend I'm writing to a dear friend about my novel, someone who is a careful reader and well-disposed to my ideas. That works for me. It might not work for anyone else, which is why I don't think step-by-step directions are helpful.

Notes

The Pitch and Why I Should Care

A pitch is the shortest of the "why my book is terrific" marketing tools. It comes in two forms: insanely short (one paragraph) and off-the-edge-of-reality insanely short (one or possibly two sentences.) The paragraph can be extracted wholesale from a query letter (or, conversely, inserted into same). The other one, the one that drives otherwise brilliant writers to tears, is also called an "elevator pitch" because it's what you say when you get into an elevator with the agent or editor of your dreams, who looks at you with mild interest and says, "What are you working on?"

I don't know why so many of us who are articulate and eloquent (all right, maybe not that fantastic, but competent) on the page turn into dithering lummocks when presented with such a golden opportunity. But we do. We're writers, after all, not stand-up comedians. Our medium of expression is the written word. That elevator moment demands that we present our work (a) in a medium utterly foreign to us; (b) at the drop of a hat. This is enough to send most of us into terrified blathers. Fortunately, editors and agents (at least those of my acquaintance) are kindly souls who understand this. They're willing to cut a writer a lot of slack. But not a lot of time. Ten seconds and the elevator door opens. That's it. They're gone. Do it right, however, and you might get invited to talk it over at lunch.

The third part of this equation, the one saving grace, is that we can prepare. That means having our one-sentence pitch nailed down, polished, and practiced.

Because a pitch is so short, it's got to go right to the heart of the *zing!* You don't have precious extra seconds to go into detailed explanations. You want maximum *wow!* factor per syllable.

For me, this process is very much like writing a title. I'm terrible at titles. Occasionally, just the right word or phrase or name will come to me fairly early in the project, but often I have to slog through the laborious process of finding it. I've been known to use working titles like The Hot Tub Novel. This is what I do to brainstorm titles—and pitches.

I sit down with pen and paper, which work better for me than the keyboard on which I write text. Over the years, I've developed a series of exercises to get my critical brain offline. One is a timed list: I set a timer for 1 minute, for instance, and have to come up with 15 titles. Rinse and repeat. Another eliminates the number requirement but keeps the timer: 10 minutes, keep the pen moving, don't go back, don't cross anything out—GO! Or eliminate the timer but increase the number: 30 titles, no repeats—GO!

Suppose a pitch sentence has two parts, a situation and a twist. Each can be drilled by the same methods used for a title.

At this point, I have generated pages of scrawl, most of which is beyond laughably bad. Usually, however, I find one or two that point me in the right direction. They may or may not be just the thing, but I've broken the mind-paralysis. I look over my candidates for vagueness ("this sounds like every other teenage vampire romance"), infelicities of word choice, or failure-to-sparkle.

The next step, unless I am certain one of them is exactly right, "a match made in heaven," is to find a trusted listener or three. They can be fellow writers or people who work in other fields where they might use a pitch themselves. Once you've gotten the written pitch down, these same friends can serve as an audience while you practice. It probably isn't necessary to recite your pitch word-perfect in real life, but you want to be so solid on the essentials that they flow trippingly from your tongue.

Now you've developed your pitch, you may fear that you will never have the chance to use it. Perhaps you don't attend conventions or writers conferences where you might meet an agent or editor. Never fear! Life will provide you with other occasions, ones you might not have noticed. Ones that, I might add, can get you invited to speak at book clubs and libraries and high school English classes, or even an interview with your college alumni magazine or local newspaper. I suspect that simply because I have that succinct *wow!* statement handy, I am much more likely to let people know I've written a book. The pitch then gives me a launching pad for a discussion (as opposed to my bumbling around, trying to express "what it's about" and missing that moment of open curiosity).

When I was a fairly new writer, with only a couple of short story sales, Poul Anderson asked me what I was working on. Gentleman that he was, he very kindly listened through what must have been the most inept pitch since the dawn of time. For no other reason than to never again abuse another writer's courteous interest, I try to have a short description of my latest story ready. It may not be a finished pitch, but it provides a succinct way of encapsulating why I'm in love with the project.

No, I won't give you examples. Unless we meet in an elevator.

INK DANCE

Notes

Book Promotion Rehabilitation

Sherwood Smith offered some thoughts on the obnoxiousness of authors tooting their own horns unrelentingly in interviews:

"Too many read as if the person was interviewing themself, examining why I'm the greatest, and my novel is the greatest, from every angle in the mirror. The interviews don't look outward, talking about other things."

This brings to mind a panel topic at Westercon not too many years ago, "How To Promote Yourself As A Writer Without Being Obnoxious." That we even need to discuss the social etiquette of career building is significant in itself. We aren't born knowing how to communicate our enthusiasm for our creative efforts. In the world of science fiction and fantasy, like any other genre, there is wide variation in social skills. Aforementioned skills are not necessary to write brilliantly, although an ability to *observe* them in others is useful. I've known writers who were so painfully shy, they'd rather undergo a root canal without anesthetic than go up to a stranger and try to convince him to buy their book, and other writers who gleefully do just that, over and over again.

Many writers would be just as happy to remain in their own little rooms, happily typing away on their stories. Once upon a time, it was much easier to let the publisher handle the publicity. Books would stay in print and in bookstores long enough for (print) reviews and word of mouth to drive sales.

The shift from that model to faster turnover (books may stay on the shelves only weeks or days or–*shudder*—hours), print runs determined by pre-orders, and the buying practices of chain bookstores (where one buyer might make the selection for many stores) have all contributed to pressure the author to take a more active or pre-emptive role in book promotion. I can't decide if the Internet, with its potential for very fast communication, makes the situation better or worse. "Generating a buzz" or "going viral" seem to have taken the place of slower, more thoughtful and personal recommendations.

I'm going to set aside the question that building up an Internet readership (as in the more popular blogs) and connections ("Mirror, mirror, on the wall, who's got the most retweets of all?") takes time and a certain knack. Instead, I'll ask, what is being promoted? A specific book? A body of work? The writer himself?

If it's a specific book, I submit it's far more effective to communicate what's cool and nifty and heartbreaking about the story itself, rather than the greatness of the book. ("Orphan goes to wizard school, where he and his friends battle trolls in bathrooms, outwit three-headed dogs, and play magical chess with life-sized pieces" is much more likely to elicit my interest than, "Harry Potter is the greatest book of all time.") This is harder when describing a body of work, but the same principle applies: specific details ("A crusader-turned-monk uses keen observation and insight into human nature to solve murders, while wrestling with internal politics at his monastery, the shifting sides of England's civil war, etc." works better than "The Brother Cadfael books are historical mysteries.")

As for the author herself, I come back to Smith's comment about looking outward and talking about things of interest. We don't write books in order to be loved; at least, I hope we don't. That's not what either writing or relationships are about. So if we set out to promote our work, it should be our work and not ourselves we are offering to the world. (The corollary here is that when a story is rejected, it's the words on the page that are being refused, not ourselves as writers or as human beings.) One of my pet peeves is authors who refer only to their own (all too often, unpublished) stories when discussing larger topics. There is a place for "stories about stories," as long as the content itself—the ideas, the adventures-in-writing—remain the focus point.

Here's Deborah's Theory of Promotion. I'm appreciative of the honor of someone reading my blog or coming to hear me on a panel or writing me an email. There's no price for admission. Instead, I try to offer something of value, whether it's my considered opinion (or my insane off-the-cuff commentary), or adventures that have meaning for me, or a free story. It's how I hold up my part of this far-flung conversational community. I believe that if you like what I have to say, you'll be more inclined to pick up one of my books. I try to make it a friendly and easy process to check out what they're about.

One of the best things about the ebook revolution is that the success of any given book, or my work in general, does not depend on what happens in the few weeks pre- and post-release. With an ebook, a readership can develop gradually and organically. I have a sense of spaciousness of time. Time in which to write my best. Time in which to develop connections with people who want to read what I love to write (and vice versa, to discover wonderful authors).

Pull up a chair. Have a cup of tea. Let's talk about books and ideas and life. And may we each come away enriched and inspired by one another.

INK DANCE

Notes

Non-Obnoxious Book Promotion, Part 2

To be honest, I don't have the answer as to what works and what doesn't. (I don't think anyone does, beyond pointing out things that are incredibly annoying, or things that have succeeded spectacularly for other people under special circumstances.) One of the worst aspects of relentless self-promotion is the gnawing insecurity it generates in others, as if failure to be spectacularly successful is your own fault. That sense of desperation is not only toxic, it's contagious. For me, a playful and cooperative approach helps defuse the pressure to follow someone else's strategy. One size does not fit all, especially at the cost of precious creative energy.

(I know what I feel comfortable with and what drives me nuts. I also am not big on rules, especially rules handed down by someone else. Whenever I read Authoritative Advice, I want to prove it wrong.) Here are a few ideas, as they pop into my brain.

If you're on a panel:

Avoid the "Wall'O'Books," a solid mass of every publication you have, often spilling over into the space of the panelists to either side. If you're next to a better-known author who merely mentions her latest release during the introductions, you'll look like an amateur and a braggart. Speaking of introductions, I heard Madeleine L'Engle say of herself on a panel: "I write books." That was it. Period. I thought, *How incredibly classy*. But then, you say, she's Madeleine L'Engle, who needs no introduction. I suspect that in many cases, the stature of the writer is in inverse relation to the number of books displayed. Most of us do well to give the audience something to go on, so wave that gorgeous cover flat and then put it down. Let the audience see your face, not a blur of covers.

Please, please don't refer to your unpublished work as if the audience already knows it. In fact, it's better not to refer to it at all, unless in the service of a greater point. (For example, research methods.) Or if someone asks you specifically what you're working on, and then do be brief.

Remember that the panel is a *conversation*, not a series of monologs. Listening and asking follow-up questions creates an even better impression than steamrollering right over the other panelists. It's useful to assume the audience has not come to hear you, they've come to hear everyone else, so the more content you can add to the discussion, the better you establish yourself as a Person With Interesting Ideas.

When encountering fans:

Perhaps the most helpful piece of advice is to give them an opening to gracefully disengage. Exert no coercion. Start by having your pitch ready and polished, acknowledge the fan's interest, and give her a way to leave if she's not interested.

"Yes, I'm a writer. My latest book is *Twitch*, a coming-of-age story in a world where the government has outlawed heterosexuality and roller skating. Are you on your way to a panel, or do you have a moment to hear more?"

"Thanks for chatting with me. Would you like a bookmark to take away?"

"I appreciate your taking the time to listen. If you're interested, Borderlands in the dealer's room has signed copies and I'd be happy to personalize one for you."

On the Internet:

Here's where I experience the greatest degree of "nobody knows what works" and "your tolerance may vary." There's so much you can do to create and develop "an Internet presence." For myself, I need to be vigilant about time and energy boundaries, or all my writing time can go into noodling around the blogosphere.

I think it's a good idea to compartmentalize: *this* is talking about my stories; *that* is talking about writing in general or politics or anything else besides my specific works. I get irate when I begin to read a post that promises to be an interesting discussion and ends up being a sales pitch. Don't bait and switch.

I like the idea of exchanging reviews, as long as they're honest opinions. Some people think it's Internet favoritism, so don't do it if you're not comfortable. If a book isn't my cup of tea, I'm likely to politely decline to comment on it, although sometimes looking at what I don't care for leads to interesting stuff, better framed in a discussion of its own. I think it's fine to approach blog reviewers and offer them review copies. (Again, having a succinct pitch is a good idea.)

A variation of the "Wall'O'Books" is the sidebar or separate page on a website or blog with publications and purchasing links. I don't find this objectionable (in fact, it's often useful), but don't put one up if you cringe when you see it.

Notes

Gatekeeping in the World of Ebooks

In this day, when social media are saturated with writers touting their self-published novels, it seems that anyone can write a book. Anyone with any talent or ambition, that is. Certainly, anyone willing to plug along and generate 80K or 100K words can do so.

On the other hand, so many of those who want to write never follow through, and of those, many never complete their project. To have finished a novel is an achievement, regardless of its quality or marketability. I think that's worth taking a moment to appreciate. We lose sight of how extraordinary this is, and we then miss out on the benefit of taking a moment to savor this accomplishment as a cause for celebration and pride in itself. Instead, we turn to publication as a source of validation. Sometimes there are intermediate steps, such as feedback from a workshop or critique group, or the search for an agent. But all too often, the next step is to format the book, slap it up on the Internet, and *voilà*, one instantly becomes a "published author."

The ease of self-publication removes the gatekeeper function formerly performed by editors and agents. This is not entirely a bad thing. Both have been wrong in the past, and marvelous works—particularly those that are "too difficult" or "too controversial" or simply do not fit into current marketing niches have had a difficult time finding a publishing home. (Case in point: *A Wrinkle In Time* by Madeleine L'Engle, which received over twenty rejections.)

However, the literary gatekeeper is not necessarily the slayer of good books. None of us has an accurate perspective on the quality and value of our work. This is true regardless of where we are in our writing careers, although it poses a stronger problem for beginning writers. After we've been at this for a while, we have a cadre of insightful, trusted beta readers and we've worked with professional editors enough to have a sense of where our own weaknesses lie. We've acquired some degree of critical skill, even though we acknowledge this may not be reliable when applied to our current darlings. We know we have blind spots, but we also have the experience to judge when a work is ready for a round of pre-submission critiques, how to listen to that feedback, the willingness to rip things apart until they work properly, and when it's time to send the thing off to an agent or editor. In other words, we ourselves set up a series of hoops to jump through, each of which is designed to help us determine, *Is this book ready for the next step?* By the time the manuscript arrives on the desk of the acquiring editor, it's likely been vetted by "a new pair of eyes" a number of times.

(There are, of course, variations to this process. If a project is sold on proposal, it's been through a differently-rigorous process at an earlier creative stage.)

Nowadays, many authors who still work with traditional print publishers also self-publish. The easy releases are the reprints of out-of-print novels that have already been through the editorial process. (And hopefully, decent copy-editing and proofreading, but that's another topic.) What about stories that got "We love it, but we can't market it" rejections? What about books yet unscrutinized by editorial eyes?

Beginning writers often lack a cohort of peers. If they are fortunate enough to be in a critique group with more experienced writers or they have established a mentorship relationship with a professional writer or editor, or if they have networked in some other way with those with more developed critical skills, then they are already well ahead of the game. They're more likely to understand where their stories are on the journey to publishable quality and what they need to do in order to improve it.

The operant phrase here is *publishable quality*. When there are no gatekeepers (aka editors), does this phrase even have meaning? Isn't it a matter of opinion, that one reader's publishable quality is another's drek (and vice versa!)? And does it matter, so long as an ebook sells? What's wrong with a situation in which anyone who's thrown together 80K or even 50K or 150K words, formats it, puts it up as a Kindle or Nook edition, promotes it all over the social media sites, and sells a bunch of copies (or a whole big bunch of copies)? Isn't that how the market works, by giving readers what they're looking for?

The problem I have with this scenario, being enacted thousands of times over the various epublishing venues, is not so much the flood of unreadable or barely-readable books making it increasingly difficult to find the ones I want. It's the disservice it does to the newer writer.

Each one of us has a unique perspective, a precious voice that is ours alone. As Edith Layton said, "No one else in the wide world, since the dawn of time, has ever seen the world as you do, or can explain it as you can. This is what you have to offer that no one else can." But we have to learn how to tell those stories in a way that fully realizes (makes real) them. To make them the best we can. We aren't born knowing how to do this. At least, I wasn't. We need practice and critical evaluation and explanation of the techniques and principles of good fiction.

Rejection of early, poorly-conceived or even more poorly-executed novels, as disheartening and aggravating as it is, teaches us patience and keeps our standards high and our egos in check. I'm not advancing the argument that because I and writers of my generation "had to suffer" through one round of obtuse rejection slips after another, that every new writer must therefore do so. I'm questioning whether eliminating the "apprenticeship/journeyman" stage of writing mastery is a good thing. And if it isn't, what is a beginning writer to do?

If all you want to do is have a virtual shelf of books to brag about, that's one thing. But if your goal is a lifelong writing *career*, with growth and development toward your full potential as a writer and with the creation of works of enduring value, then you would do well to replicate the educational process in your own work. This might be through peer-run writers groups, workshops at conventions in which you receive critiques from established writers, formal courses such as Clarion/Clarion West, Viable Paradise, or similar workshops, or one-on-one mentorship with a writer or freelance editor (I think this latter is one of the most exciting developments in learning-to-write, with the opportunity to work closely with a seasoned professional).

One of the hardest things for a newer writer to accept is that not every early attempt at a novel is successful. Furthermore, heavily promoting an *unsuccessful* novel is one of the surest ways of sabotaging a career before it gets off the ground. We really, really don't want to concede that the darling we have labored so hard over is, not to put too fine a point on it, utterly dreadful. The way through that agonizing stage is to keep working at your craft, write another book with a completely new concept and characters, keep pushing yourself, get the best critical feedback you can, write another book and another. At some point, you will be able to look back and see for yourself why that first attempt didn't work. If you keep at it, you'll also notice when your stories started to soar. That's the threshold! That's when it's time to send the book out to agent or editor, or to consider the self-publication route. How you decide on one or the other is complex and rife with highly opinionated arguments one way or the other. The important thing is to become your own gatekeeper… with a lot of help from your friends.

Notes

Story and Self

Juliette Wade presents some interesting thoughts on self and story in the context of the revision process. She makes the point that your story isn't you. Here's what I think about different ways of looking at the relationship:

1. Your Story Is You. Many of us have had the experience of being so enmeshed in a story (or characters) that we just can't hear criticism of the words on the page as distinct from a personal attack. Sometimes it's because we see so much of ourselves in the characters. They are, after all, having the adventures we wish we could have, or they are the people we wish we were. So we develop a selective blindness about them as characters, often in terms of inconsistent motivation, lack of significant shortcomings, or perhaps even the reverse, mistakes that don't make sense (a la Italian opera plots).

There's a corollary for plot and story, in which our original idea is so precious to us that we twist and turn and distort and jam illogical things together to make everything come together "the way it has to happen." Sometimes that story we're reaching for really is the right one; more often, however, we start with a flawed or superficial conception and develop it into something solid in the process of getting rid of whatever doesn't work. I'm talking about the sense of inviolability, of plot being "darling" in the sense of non-negotiable as an extension of ego/self.

2. Your Story Is Words On The Page. This is the conventional view advanced in writing workshops, critique groups, and panels on writing. It's immensely helpful in establishing distance between you—a person, a writer of many stories—and this specific piece of work. That makes it easier to hear feedback about what you actually wrote, not what you envisioned or thought you wrote. (As a side note, one of the reasons it's hard to copy-edit

your own work is that we see what we intended, not necessarily what's on the page.) Sometimes, getting from story-as-self to story-as-words-on-page feels like a divorce, a death, a beloved child leaving home. Other times, it's a relief. *Oh, I did a horrible job with the story I meant to tell, but there's an even better story buried under the drek.* Which, I admit, is how almost all of my early stories worked.

3. Your Story Has A Life Of Its Own. I think we all run into this when a story "comes to life" and runs away with us, when the words just pour out, or when characters develop minds of their own and do unexpected things (that often don't fit with our preconceived notions of plot!) We joke about secondary characters threatening to take over the entire story, or demanding books of their own. Janni Lee Simner often blogs about delightful conversations with her characters. This view of story is a double-edged sword. On the one hand, it's exhilarating to surf on the wave of unfolding story, one of the best highs there is. All kinds of wonderful things result. Sometimes, we like those pushy, opinionated secondary characters better than the tepid heroes. Then there's nothing to do but tear the story apart and put it together with the right focus.

On the other hand, if we look at the story as a sort of Platonic Ideal Form, existing as an integral whole outside of us, it can be much harder to make substantial changes. It's easy to glamorize the struggles of an artist, and actually, it's a form of boasting to agonize publicly about the vividness of our creations and the recalcitrance (realness) of our characters. I know I'm going to get people upset with me, but I think when we say, "I can't make my character do what I want her to," it's admitting to lazy writing. A poorly executed, inconsistent, un-thought-out character is going to feel as if she's talking back or "has a mind of his own." Then, instead of doing the hard work of developing a deep, complex character in relationship with other multidimensional, idiosyncratic characters, we just throw up our hands. After all, if the characters truly do exist independently of us, we stand as much chance of changing them as we might trying to get an alcoholic to stop drinking. That way lies madness.

Notes

Stages in a Writer's Development

Beginning writers (and experienced ones, too) are often possessed—haunted, really—by the notion that we already know how to write. While few insist that this is something instinctive that we were born with, there's a persistent and pernicious belief that "talent" will automatically produce great literature... or at least commercially successful work. I lay much of the blame for this on our education. We learned how to write in elementary school, didn't we? We turned in all those school papers, essays, book reports, didn't we? We write every day—shopping lists, emails, text messages, don't we? So how hard can it be to write a book? It's just a longer version of LOL, BRB, isn't it?

Even if we come to understand that professional writing, whether fiction or non-, whether mainstream or genre or poetry, requires skill, and skill comes about through understanding and practice, all too often we don't give ourselves full credit for being able to grow. How often have I wailed, "I'll never get any better!" when in fact I am on the brink of a quantum leap forward in the scope and richness of my story-telling?

In his excellent book, *Creating Short Fiction*, Damon Knight describes stages in a writer's development. The very notion is extraordinary. Assuming we are willing to work at acquiring and perfecting the skills necessary for good writing, we need to understand that growth is not uniform. A larva is not a caterpillar is not a chrysalis is not a butterfly. Some issues may always plague us—our "writing nemesis" sort of stuff—but our focus will change along with our development.

Here's Damon's breakdown:

Stage 1: Writing to please yourself, mostly day-dream, self-indulgent stories. A lot of fanfic falls here. You really don't care whether anyone else reads it because you're your own audience.

Stage 2. You care about an audience, but your stories are what Damon calls, "trivial," that is, lacking in storyness, in emotional and structural shape. At this stage, it occurs to you that you might want to learn something about what makes stories work.

Stage 3. Now you're writing complete stories or, as Damon puts it, "reasonable imitations," but still face serious challenges in terms of technique and execution. Often these weaknesses pertain to characterization or overall story structure/balance.

Stage 4. You're working at a professional level, with reasonable control over all the basics. This is an open-ended stage because hopefully we never stop learning, never stop "pushing the envelope" for our work.

There is absolutely nothing wrong with being at any of these stages or remaining there if that's what you want to do with your writing. Most, but not all, successful writers have passed this way. You're in good company.

Understanding where you are, looking around at the territory behind and ahead of you, can be immensely reassuring. It can help you analyze and focus on the learning challenges of where you are. I still dream up Stage 1 stories, but I know that's what they are… pure self-indulgence. Many times, ideas will leap out at me and say, "I belong in a real story." I know what to do with them because I've slogged through Stages 2 and up. If I didn't, if I were still a beginner, I'd look at that moment as a sign of readiness, an invitation to push forward, an impulse to take a step up that next rung of the ladder.

So where does Mary Sue (or Gary Stu) fit in? The term is often used dismissively to describe a character, usually in fanfic, who is a thinly-disguised representation of the author, in many ways, "the author's pet." She or he can be wonderful beyond belief, or equally unbelievably ordinary, but every other character of the appropriately attractive gender falls madly in love with her/him.

The implication is that because such characters and stories are wish-fulfillment, they are without value. Or that writers who indulge themselves in this way are immature and unprofessional.

In dismissing "Mary Sue/Gary Stu stories," we risk cutting ourselves off from the creative wellspring that fuels them. As children, we all daydreamed Mary Sue (and Gary Stu) stories—we all wanted to be heroes and have wonderful adventures. As we grew up, our notions about what constitutes a wonderful adventure may have changed. We may still want to go flying on a dragon, but now we also want that devilishly handsome (or intoxicatingly beautiful) dragon-rider to fall in love with us.

Mary Sue/Gary Stu daydreams allow us to explore that landscape of yearning, to figure out what lights us up with wonder and delight (or lust). If we react to our "guilty pleasure" daydreams with scorn, we can never learn what they have to teach us. These characters, situations, and worlds bring passion and meaning to our work.

As we progress in our development as writers, we learn to take the raw stuff and refine it, plaster our heroes with warts, apply our professional critical skills, and take the story in unexpected and interesting directions.

Without Mary Sue, without those "idle" longings, guilty pleasures, and crazed desires for escape to the world of our dreams, however, all we've got is the warts.

Notes

Blackberry Writing

Blackberries are tricksy things. They can look ripe from where I stand, but turn out to be all red at the base. Sometimes I can tell the moment I touch the berry—it's too firm and too tightly attached to the stem. I have to be ready to give up on what looked like a great prospect and move on. When I'm in the flow of picking, it seems I don't even have to think about this. Isn't this like a story that seems promising but doesn't yet have the necessary depth? Occasionally—well, more than occasionally—my mind gets dead set on "this berry gets picked" and I force the issue. I'll glare at the red parts and either pop the berry into my mouth ("for private reading only"). Berries that are almost-ready go well in oatmeal. I freeze quarts and quarts of them for winter breakfasts. They're too sour on their own, but they blend well, adding pleasantly tart notes. That's not unlike taking several different story ideas, none of which can stand on their own, and setting them at cross-purposes to make a much more interesting tale.

This whole business of "readiness" in a story is a curious one. It's a bit like cooking without a recipe, because while there may be guidelines, there are no hard and fast rules of how to tell when a story concept is "ripe."

Editor Laura Anne Gilman talks describes how unprofessional it is to argue with a rejection:

All too often at the Big NYC Publisher's Office, after rejecting a work — especially if it was a) slush and b) got our standard slush reject letter, which was polite but clear that it wasn't something we were interested in— we'd get a response from the submitter.

Now, professionals know that, unless you are specifically invited into an exchange, you don't respond to a rejection. You take it, you consider what's worth considering, and you move on. That exchange is over.

Sometimes, the response would be to ask for more details. Time-crunches didn't allow us to do that, but it was an acceptable if frustrating response.

More often, though, we got a response along the lines of "My work is utter genius, and you're too blinded by (fill in the blank) to see it! But you'll be sorry!"

This kind of reaction isn't limited to beginning writers, but it is an insidious trap. It's far easier to think that your story got rejected because of the blindness/stupidity/conspiracy of the gatekeepers, rather than that it simply isn't good enough. It could be a great idea and you weren't ready to do it any kind of justice. It could be a trivial idea that no writer alive could have turned into a decent story. It could have been a nifty idea but it wasn't properly developed—it wasn't "ripe."

One of the hardest things for a new writer to master is accepting that there is a threshold of quality—for ideas, for execution—for publication. It's hard to hear that the story you are so proud of isn't good enough. Those thorns hurt as much when I'm pulling out as when I'm pushing in.

Here's the catch: sometimes the story is great. Sometimes the market just isn't ready for the story at this time, but it will be in the future. Somewhere there's an editor and a readership who will adore it. How can you tell?

Experienced writers usually get a sense of whether a story is a passing tone in music, more valuable for where it gets you than for itself, best set aside as an interesting but unsuccessful experiment, or whether it is worthy of continued confidence. I can't say *no beginning writers* have this maturity of perspective, but I think it extraordinarily unlikely. It comes with trial and error and constant critical attention to the work. It comes with patience, and it offers more patience as the payoff.

So what is a beginning writer, or a middling writer, or any writer, to do? Here are some immediate thoughts, but everyone's solution is going to be different and to change with time.

Get lots of support, people who share a vision of a career as being long-term, hopefully life-long. While striving to make each new project the best you can, keep perspective. Yes, there are "break-out" books, but what makes or a breaks a career is steady improvement. Most of us, on occasion, need shoulders to cry on, hands to hold, friends to celebrate with, and colleagues with contagious enthusiasm for writing itself.

Beware the lure of self-publishing. It definitely has its place, but it ought not to substitute for inadequate quality by providing a way around the traditional gatekeepers. While it is remotely possible that an early work might be not right for today's larger market but perfect for a specific, smaller readership (and hence a good candidate for self-publishing), it is far more likely it simply hasn't passed that threshold of quality. Assume it hasn't. Work harder, write better, and keep pushing your critical skills and your standards.

Notes

When A Story Isn't Ready, Part 2

Most writers who have been at this business for any length of time have the experience of a story not being truly finished. It may come to an end, but it has not yet come into itself. My version of this usually involves my initial concept being wrong. I will start with an idea in what I call the "front part" of my brain—a notion, a conceit, an image from some visual medium (painting, film) and spin it into a plot. I labor under the delusion that this is what the story "is about." More often than not, I'm wrong.

I'm wrong because I'm going for the glitz, the superficial attraction. The truth is, I'm a better writer than that when I listen to what's underneath the glitz. That's where the emotional juice is, the deeper resonances, the Deborah-vision.

The symptoms of this mis-step are many: characters that refuse to follow the pre-arranged script, story elements that just won't come together, plot idiocies that are not just holes but dead-end canyons. I've learned to rip all that stuff out (leaving chunks of bleeding, burning manuscript strewn about) and dig deep into the core. That's part of my revision (re-vision, right?) process. Although with time (read: decades of practice), I've gotten better at writing first drafts that are less superficial and more true, I still value this process. Throw away the chaff; be ruthless; seek the nuggets of treasure and bring them into the light.

Stories can be not ready in other ways, too. You throw them in the infamous trunk when you're so tired of looking at the same words, you can't see the problems you know are there. I've been known to put manuscripts in the freezer to cool them off, although I doubt the physical temperature has any effect except as a metaphor. Working on something else gives "the back" of our brains time to work, for ideas to ferment and percolate and for new patterns and solutions to emerge. Alas, this process can take years, which is why it's a good idea to immediately dive into the next project and the next.

Sometimes it's me, the writer, who's not ready to tell that story. Usually this is because my writing craft isn't adequate to the challenge. This is particularly true if the story is a "high wire act," requiring great skill and subtlety. Or a story that plays into my weaknesses as a writer and refuses to be told in any other way. Or something I myself am not ready to tackle, like emotionally difficult subjects.

If I try to write these stories before I'm ready, they will fail just as surely as those I first described. Perhaps every failed story involves elements of story-unfinished-ness and my own imperfect skill. However, I've found that the attempt is always valuable. If I am willing to listen to the heart of the story and to see myself as being a work-in-progress, then I will surely receive priceless gifts. I grow as a person as well as a writer, and end up with stories I am proud of.

Notes

Series as Career Killer

Sometimes when we create a world, whether it is for a novel or a shorter piece, we realize how much of it exists "off the page" and we come to love it so much we want to go explore. Or to stay in the same location or time period and delve more deeply into it. Or simply to run away to our favorite imaginary place with our favorite characters. These multi-novel variations allow us to do that, to create related stories, to use and build upon our vision of a world. Incidentally, I have been known to bribe secondary characters who are threatening to run away with the plot with the promise of their very own stories. Knowing that I can "spin off" such tales helps me to focus on this story, to keep plot and subplot from burgeoning into a shapeless and planet-consuming proteus. Sometimes I find that secondary characters or places mentioned only in passing turn out to be more interesting, more complex and ambivalent, dark and transcendent, than my original conceptions.

The pitfall of writing a series when a writer is still new and learning craft is that working in an established world means we don't create new ones, and world-building is a skill that improves with practice. If your first story is the only one you ever want to write, that's less of a problem than if you are like me and your head is filled with a gazillion story ideas, each screaming to be told. I think you do yourself a disservice in committing years of your formative literary life to one vision, instead of pushing to make each new world more complex and fascinating. One of the benefits of writing short fiction is the relatively small time investment in each story, as compared to working at novel length. Mistakes cost a far smaller fraction of your overall career, and each story is an opportunity to start fresh, aim higher, and twist reality in a different way.

Notes

How Gossip Can Trash Your Writing Career

Volumes have been written about ways to offend a prospective agent or editor: unprofessional queries, manuscripts printed in purple ink on yellow paper in Gothic font, annoying phone calls, even stalking. The story of the manuscript pushed under the door of the toilet stall is legendary. These tactics backfire, and not just because they are obnoxious and immediately communicate that the writer has not a clue about publishing protocol and appropriate behavior. They constitute an abuse of the agent's or editor's time (and eyesight).

Editors and agents are, it goes without saying, human beings with hopes and dreams, families and outside problems. They have good days, bad days, and times they use less than perfect judgment. Most of them love their work and want to love ours. Now more than ever, the publishing industry is under tremendous pressure—*implosion* might be a more apt description. In addition to their regular duties, most editors find themselves staggering under the burden of more and more non-editorial work, not to mention worrying about how they're going to buy groceries if the firm goes belly-up. *Anything* that a writer does that adds to the crap level in an editor's life must raise the question, "Is this worth the hassle, when there are a dozen equally promising projects that don't come with strings?"

So you study the business, you present your manuscript in the prescribed format, manner, and place. You communicate in a timely, appropriate, and courteous manner. You even buy your editor a drink at WorldCon. Things are going great! Maybe you've got an offer or a multi-volume contract, or a book or five under your belt. Your agent returns your calls; you're on a first-name basis with your editor. What can go wrong? Besides the vagaries of the market, the whims of distributors, and such like?

Picture this: You're at a major con, at a late night room party with a group of editorial type folk, some of whom are not entirely sober, most of whom are jet-lagged, and all of whom are overdue for serious relaxation time. One of them lets slip a hilarious but less-than-flattering reference to an author past/present/slushpile.

You:

A. Whip out your cellphone and text all your friends, because why keep a good joke to yourself?

B. Post *What She Said* on Twitter, complete with names, dates and places.

C. Make a mental note to email the editor on the next business day, with the hint that you will be more than happy to keep this information secret in exchange for a favor or two.

D. Instantly develop amnesia on the subject. If any reference to the party arises, look sheepish and mumble, "I was so tired, I can't remember much, but it was a great party."

Look, editors and agents and suchlike folk are people, genre publishing is a small world, and very little stays secret. Unless there's a credible threat of physical violence necessitating immediate police intervention, let it go. You won't score any brownie points by becoming the fount of the latest buzz. On the other hand, you might harm someone, including the person who let slip the tale.

Will it hurt your book's chances of a sale and decent promotion if you repeat embarrassing details? Is gossip a professional black mark? Nope, your book will rise or fall on its merits, and everyone understands the human temptation to Pass On The Juicy News.

Will your editor think twice before calling you with a secret, rush project? Will you get invited to the next round of let-down-your-hair parties? Perhaps ones at which anthologies or shared-world series are hatched and invitations issued?

How would you feel if you repeated a story that, whether true or not, damaged someone's reputation, someone you might find yourself wanting to work with in the future? Writers become editors and vice versa, editors change publishing houses, writers become publishers, editors become agents, writers collaborate and form online ventures.

And that writer you heard the story about, the story you expunged from your memory—he might just turn out to be your best ever writing buddy.

Note: A version of this essay appeared in 2010 as part of the "How To Trash Your Writing Career" series on Book View Café.

Notes

Reviews: The Good, the Bad, and the Ignorable

A friend who recently published her second mystery novel (published, as in a New York publisher and a respectable one at that) lamented online how difficult and anxiety-provoking it was for her to read reviews of her work.

While anticipating her first novel appearing in the bookstores, she suffered, "visions of humiliation, public contempt, vicious attacks on my writing, plot, and [background] information. I slept poorly and contemplated changing my name and moving to Belize."

This person is an adult, an accomplished professional, and had done her authorial homework. She'd had solid workshop experience in addition to a rigorous academic background, so she was no stranger to feedback. What is it about reviews that can turn the most secure of us into quivering jellyfish (swimming toward Belize)? Why do we give them such power over us?

After all, anyone can write a review these days. No training or experience—or taste or perspicacity—are required. Just look at the reader reviews on Amazon.com or similar sites. Blog reviews range from insightful to malicious to blindly adoring. Nor is it necessary to have actually read the book in question. I stumbled upon a review of *Lace and Blade 2* (an anthology I edited) several months before it was to be released (and since the book was Print on Demand, no ARCs had yet been sent out and no one but the publisher and me had seen the final manuscript). The review: "Not very good." Since I knew the reviewer could not possibly have read it, I had to ask, why post such a comment? Simply to strew the Internet with negativity? To pose as knowing everything about everything? A personal vendetta against me, the publisher, or one of the authors?

The generic nature of the comment offers a clue. Amateur reviewers can be thoughtful, articulate, and fair-minded. But they can also use the vehicle of the Internet to disguise their personal agendas. I saw this in the comments about a recently-published book from a small press that dealt (with imagination and humor, I thought) with a controversial theme. Some reviewers had the honesty to say, "This was not my cup of tea" or "I disagree with the underlying premise." But others simply said "It's a bad book" with so little explanation that the remark could have been applied equally well to James Joyce's *Ulysses*, the *Kama Sutra*, and an unabridged Mongolian-French dictionary.

Had it been my own work in question (and at times, it has been), I would no doubt have taken the generic judgment at face value. However, this instance and subsequent discussion led to a different perspective: all too often, reviewers react to their own personal shortcomings by denigrating whatever sets them off. Today's world does not lack for hot-button issues and personal grudges.

Of course, not all negative reviews are based on unconsidered personal prejudice towards the subject material (or even the author). A member of a writer's workshop used to occasionally preface remarks with "Normally, I would rather walk barefoot over hot coals than read this type of fiction," and then proceed to give a reasoned, intelligent, and helpful critique. I might go so far as to say that a review that does not discuss a book's weaknesses is likely to be superficial at best.

Regardless of the value of negative commentary, is it useful for the author to read such reviews? For that matter, is it useful for an author to read reviews that are unadulterated glowing praise? I suggest that it is not.

Most people seek approval and bask in adulation, and writers are no different. We want to be told we've done well, that our words are glorious, timeless, stupendously wonderful, stunning, rousing, awesome, terrific, and any number of the phrases so casually thrown about. The bottom line is that we can get all this and more from our dogs.

The question is: does unconsidered praise help us to become better writers? Does pointless and mean-spirited book bashing help us to become better writers?

If it doesn't, are we helping or hurting ourselves by reading either type of review?

It is helpful when learning the craft of writing to know what has worked or not for a reader. Often the most valuable form of critique for me runs along the lines of, "You lost me here."

To write, we have to do just the opposite. We have to turn away from external feedback and listen to our inner voices, to discern those visions that are ours alone. Praise, because it is pleasurable, is particularly potent and difficult to disregard. Therefore, it poses a greater threat to the creative process than does outright criticism. Yes, some beginning writers crumble under harsh feedback and never write again. But even more of us shape our work and distort our vision because of praise.

This is why many writers won't show anyone their works-in-progress. The stories are not yet fully formed, and are therefore vulnerable to someone else's opinion. So what's the harm in reading reviews, once the story is published? Hopefully, that story will not be your last.

Reviews, whether positive or negative, persist in the writer's mind. If we have only so many years in which to spin out the stories of our hearts, can we afford even the ghost of a distraction, not to mention the hours of anguish, insomnia, and thoughts of Belize?

We are all human. I have no expectation that I, or anyone who reads this, will successfully resist reading reviews. I hope, however, that we will take what they say cautiously, mindfully, ever aware of their illusory seduction… and then set them aside as best we can and get on with our real work.

Notes

Surviving Dry Spells

L aura Anne Gilman offers some savvy perspective on surviving the dry spells:

Remember, a few weeks ago, when I said that every career has its ups and downs? That not even bestsellers hit it out of the park every time? Awards don't always equal sales, sales aren't always enough, readers' tastes change, and so do publishers. Careers rise—and they fall.

Sometimes it's obvious. Sometimes it's not. You might keep working, but at lower advances to match lower sales. Or you might not be able to sell another book, no matter how good, how smart, how interesting the books are.

We all need the reminder that publishing is cyclical and that many elements are beyond our control. We needs ways of staying in touch with why we became writers in the first place. We also need survival strategies so we can pay the bills, whether we get unrelated day jobs or not.

Years ago, Marion Zimmer Bradley said something to me in passing, only a few words, but they stuck with me. She said that along with her current commercial novel, she was writing something for her own pleasure. Most of us began writing because we loved it, and we wrote the stories we wanted to read. Our secret delights. One of the pitfalls of professional publishing is that we risk turning off that part of our writing minds. We chase the market instead of delighting our inner readers. And yet those inner readers can be our best allies during hard times. Along with fellow writers who have been there and lived to tell the tale.

Epublishing, self-publishing, are game-changers. At least, I think they are. But what do I know? I have so little sense of the market, it's pathetic. I know what I love to read and it isn't always what sells. However, one thing I am reasonably sure of: publishing is in flux, and we don't know how it's all going to fall out. Gilman talks about a dry spell as a creative opportunity; new methods of publishing open doors. That's one reason that ventures like Book View Café, an online author's cooperative, where established pro writers and editors can pool their talents, publishing not only out-of-print treasures but new material, are so exciting.

Notes

The Magic Phone Call

It's the moment every struggling-to-break-in writer dreams about. You've sweated through revision after revision, you've endured and celebrated the feedback from your critique group or trusted reader. You've haunted your own Inbox, dreading and hoping at the same time. To your query, the editor or agent replies, "Yes, we received it. Yes, it's still under consideration."

Still? Calloo callay! Agony of agonies…

The waiting comes to an end, as all things must. This time, it's not with a form rejection or even the more personalized, encouraging "almost there" notes you've been getting. It's a phone call! Is there ever a time when you most want to be cool and collected, to savor each microsecond, and yet find your brain inhabited by swarms of frantic, deafening flying things? To quote one of my daughters' favorite books: "What do you say, dear?"

Times have changed since I found myself on the receiving end of such a glorious call. Conversations used telephone or postal mail, not email. Conventional wisdom has swung away from "first sell, then get an agent." However, I believe the advice I was given and the ways in which I am happy I responded still apply.

First of all, I was of the "sell first, then agent" school. I did not and still do not believe that it is impossible to sell a first novel without an agent. You don't have to agree with me; after all, I could be wrong. I also believed that I could get a much better agent—in fact, the agent of my dreams—if I began with a novel for which an offer (from a major publisher) had already been made. It didn't bother me in the least that an agent would pocket his or her commission without marketing the book. I know myself well enough to be confident I am right up there with the world's ten lousiest negotiators. I also wanted an agent who would take the long view, not a single novel sale but my future long-term career.

When that magic phone call came, I had done considerable homework. I regularly read essays by various agents in trade magazines (now you can read their blogs online). I met writers I admired and, after sufficient friendliness and trust was established, asked them about their experiences with agents. I wasn't specifically looking for horror stories, but a sense of each agent's philosophy, the way he or she interacted with authors. I considered how similar my work was to that of the other writer. I composed my dream list. And waited. And submitted. And waited some more. And wrote several more novels while waiting.

At last came a call from my editor. "I've finished reading your book," she said. "I love your work."

Pause.

I squeaked, "Does this mean... " Oh god, I'm going to sound *so* stupid if I'm wrong! "... you want to buy it?"

She laughed.

The world turned inside out. Oops, I have to be careful saying that around fantasy and science fiction readers. It might have a literal meaning. But you get my point. With very little oxygen reaching my brain, I stammered, "This is so wonderful, I can hardly breathe. I'm so glad you like it! I can't think about numbers... you'll have to discuss that with my agent."

"Great. Have him call me."

In stupefaction, I hung up the phone. What had I done? I didn't have an agent! All I knew was not to commit to any contract specifics.

I picked up the phone and dialed the office of the agent at the top of my list. He was in. He was happy to take my call. "I've just gotten an offer from Publisher for my first novel," I said. "I've heard wonderful things about you from Author A, Author B, and Author C. Could you... er, um... negotiate the contract for me?"

"Only if we establish agent-author representation. For all your books."

"Oh. Yes, please."

Then he laughed. Although I'm delirious with joy, I'm feeling a bit idiotic. Why is everyone laughing at me?

It turned out that those same authors had been telling him about me, and he'd been waiting until I had a finished book that he could represent.

Lessons: Do your homework. Learn the field. Keep writing while you wait. Respect your strengths and weaknesses. Be friendly. And never *ever* negotiate with your brain on endorphins.

Notes

Letting Go, Moving On

One of the most difficult situations faced by any writer who is serious about being a professional is when a project never sells. It could be a short story or a novel or a series. It could happen early in your career or after you've established yourself with a solid sales record. If it hasn't happened to you, it will.

Almost all beginning writers try stories that don't work (not even counting those we don't finish!) We send them out and receive form rejection letters, with no clue as to why our stories weren't accepted or how to improve them. Unless the editor is exceptionally dedicated to encouraging new writers (Marion Zimmer Bradley was legendary for explaining why she rejected stories), they simply don't have time for individual responses. Moreover, it's not the job of an acquiring editor to critique submissions. Jokes about what to do with the ever-increasing pile of rejection letters abound. The best thing I heard about the can't-sell-anything stage was that if I was not stacking up rejection letters, I wasn't doing my job. Frustrating as it is, this experience has something valuable to teach us: Lesson One: Not Every Story Sells.

By far, the vast majority of these early rejections are due to the stories themselves. There's a threshold of quality for publication-level writing (and it has changed over time). Reaching that level does not guarantee a sale, of course. It's a necessary but not sufficient factor. This is hard to hear when we're first starting out; we're in love with our stories and can't imagine why everyone else does not feel the same way. (This is an excellent reason not to use your doting Aunt Betty for feedback. You want your delusions shattered, not inflated.) Lesson One, Subset One: Not Every Story You Write Will Be Good Enough.

Part of a writer's maturation process is accepting that sometimes you hit the mark and sometimes you don't. You do the best you can with each story, striving to make each one better. With each flop (and also with each success, when it comes), you take what you've learned and use it to tackle the next story. The worst thing you can do is to write a whole novel based on an unsuccessful short story (or a sequel or series based on an unsalable novel). If the foundation is faulty or weak, the entire structure cannot be any better. Lesson One, Subset Two: Don't Try To Build Your Career On Crap.

If this sounds harsh, it's because of how painful it is to let go of those early efforts. Nobody wants to hear that. These stories are our dreams, our darlings, the children of our minds. I've known authors who spend years and years—decades, even—on that first novel. Sometimes by the time they finish they've improved enough so they stand a chance of writing a new novel of publishable quality. But they're welded to the meandering, overwritten, inconsistent, self-indulgent screed they've poured so much work into. Even worse, they may have committed themselves to its sequel/s. They work and re-work that first novel instead of going on to something fresh, something that reflects everything they've learned. It's like trying to revise a fourth-grade essay into a doctoral dissertation.

Some stories stay in the trunk forever, and deservedly so. Others come back to tease us. I joke that my early novels are a treasure-trove of short story ideas. It is also possible for an experienced author to take an early attempt, rewrite it to their current level of skill, and have something worthwhile. It takes a high level of critical judgment, not to mention ruthlessness, to be able to do that, and almost always a substantial amount of time must elapse for the necessary detachment.

What works? What doesn't? When we're early in the learning curve, we can't tell. That's why outside feedback, whether from rejection letters, critique groups, or a paid mentor, is so valuable. These people can give us a measure of where that story is with respect to that threshold for professional publication. However, the hard part, the clawing-out-your-heart part, is up to us. We have to take those failures and set them aside. Grieve, sing a dirge, burn them, do whatever we need to do to let go. Moving on to the next story and then the next is how we grow.

At some point, we'll have a story that isn't selling but in which we—in our more-mature professional judgment—still believe. Sometimes, rejections are no-fault. The story is perfectly good but for some reason beyond our control, it doesn't fit the market. I've gotten my share of notes along the lines of, "I like this story, but I just bought one like it from Big Name Author." Other times, the market itself has changed. What was hot yesterday is unsellable today. We may have written the world's most brilliant Regency romance or space opera or angst-ridden teenage vampire novel, but no one in New York wants it if the sales figures for that particular type of story are dismal. Similarly, no publisher may be willing to take a chance on something that's too different, no matter how well-written it is.

What do you do when you're sure this book is not merely good, but the best thing you've ever written? Before electronic publishing made self-publication inexpensive, you didn't have much choice. You cried, you wept, you muttered curses at everyone from your agent to the owners of the chain bookstores…and you set it aside in the hopes that market conditions would change. This has happened many times. Change is the one constant in life. Lesson Two: Patience Prevails.

The operant phrase is an echo of what you do with a trunk story. You wrench that wonderful story out of your mind and you set it aside. You work on the next project, perhaps in a different genre. You go on.

Epublishing has changed the game because now you have the option of bringing out that hard science fiction novel or cozy steampunk mystery or police dog story yourself. Tempting as this is—and it is often a great idea—I want to insert a word of caution. The very ease of epublication has the potential to lower that professional-quality threshold. Yes, that book may not have sold because it was unusual or the timing was unfortunate, but it may also not have been competitive in quality. When we bring out books that don't fit the narrow confines of traditional print publishers, we owe it to our readers and ourselves to carefully discern whether the stories are truly the best we can offer. This is never easy, even for those of us who have been in the business a long time. That's why we need editors and colleagues to "keep us honest."

Notes

The Writer's Life

Where do you write?

Non-writers often have wildly romantic and equally wildly unrealistic visions of how we work. Or rather, where we work.

"If only," sighs the aspiring writer, "I had a cottage on the beach, a mountain getaway, an office... "

In your dreams, the working writer sniggers.

Well, yes and no. The bottom line is that if you are driven to write, you will find a way to do it, regardless of convenience or preferences. We all agree it would be wonderful to have a comfortable space, state-of-the-art computer equipment, an environment free from noise and interruptions, perhaps with an inspiring view of natural grandeur. If we put our writing career on hold until we have such a place, chances are we will never get anything written. Life doesn't often provide us with such luxuries, and they are indeed luxuries. Writing is a function of internal drive, not external setting.

I've written on a typewriter on a rickety table in the corner of the living room or longhand in a spiral notebook sitting on the floor in the same room as my kid's karate class. When I was in high school, my idea of hanging out with my friend was to sit on her bed, each of us with a portable manual typewriter, pounding away at our stories.

Technology has given us more choices in location as well as medium. I've hauled my first, incredibly heavy laptop into doctor's waiting rooms, coffee shops (this seems to be a common strategy), libraries (ditto), hotel rooms, and more. A netbook gives me even greater mobility with its lighter weight and brighter screen. These devices are conveniences, not necessities.

I've noticed over the years that I go through phases of preferring one location over another: the stability of a desk and desktop computer; the portability of a netbook, the insulation of a room with a closed door, the expansiveness of being outdoors. I rarely stick with any one place exclusively. I find that changing locale is not only good for me ergonomically but is mentally refreshing. I get a "different view" on the story in question. I like to move around, muttering under my breath, when I hit a rough patch (and woe betide any family member who mistakes this for not-working!)

I live in a very beautiful place (a sunny meadow surrounded by redwood forest) and in good weather my afternoon writing sessions take place outdoors, on the back porch beside a cascade of blooming roses. However, I must constantly remind myself that as pleasurable as this is, it is in no way essential. The moment it becomes a distraction, I need to take myself back inside or off to the library, anywhere that will re-direct my focus to what is really important—getting that story down on paper or phosphors. If I allow my ability to write to become dependent on the weather, I am setting myself up for disaster. (On the other hand, it is lovely to have access to a quiet spot while my husband is practicing his clarinet in the next room!)

Sometimes, I'm more focused and less distractible than at other times. I like to phrase it that way instead of "scatter-brained and hair-triggered." While it's helpful to be able to move to a quieter or less perturbing environment, I need to be mindful that it is not where I write, or with what medium, but the priority I give to my work that makes the difference.

Notes

Writing without Electricity

Winter storms bring power failures on a regular basis to my neck of the woods. Despite the best efforts of the CalTrans tree trimmers, branches will fall, trees will topple, and mud will slide. The neighborhood of my first house, where I lived as a single working mom, once went without power for three weeks during a previous winter. The story is that after a couple of days without refrigeration, everyone got together for a huge barbecue. Alas, I missed it, for it was before I moved there. I think the longest I went *sans* electricity was a week. My daughter, our Japanese exchange student, and I survived pretty well with flashlights and candles and oil lamps, the propane fireplace for heat, and showers at the home of my day-job supervisor.

When my husband and I bought our current house, one of the first things he did was to install a 10 kW standby generator. I attributed this action to testosterone poisoning, although I did appreciate "all the conveniences" the next time the inevitable happened. However, no system is foolproof, and the generator battery failed one winter just before it was due for its yearly maintenance. We had an interesting couple of days (wood fireplace, aforementioned lamps, etc.) but what struck me most about that experience was how many things I love to do that don't require electricity: read, play my piano, walk the dog, snuggle with my sweetie, work in the garden, knit socks…and write. That got me thinking about power failures and where power comes from.

The power to tell stories doesn't come from electricity or teachers or publishers, but sometimes I act as if it does. I come up with all kinds of excuses for not settling to write. It's too hot, it's too cold, I'm hungry, I'm sleepy, I'm restless, this book will never be any good… *Ack! The power's out! I can't use my computer!*

I learned to write stories in longhand and can still return to that medium without difficulty. I use it when I'm stuck on a scene because the kinesthetic and tactile experience of pen moving over paper involves my brain on a different level than keys going clickity-click. Not everyone makes that switch easily, and that's okay. We're all different. But generating pages is only one aspect of writing, the one most vulnerable to power outages.

One of the limitations of production quotas (so many pages per day, a novel in a month, that sort of thing) is that so many other "pieces" of writing don't involve putting words on the page. When I worked a full-time day job, I'd walk during my lunch hour. I'd plan out the next scene—or the scene I was most interested in at the moment—recite lines of dialog aloud, and act out the parts. In other words, I'd play. Have fun with it. Discover bits of detail and twists of action that I had no idea were there. A beautiful day and a winding road through successive groves of oak, eucalyptus and redwood (my lunchtime route) made this experience pleasant, but were by no means necessary—you can do it anywhere. Just exercise discretion about the reciting dialog aloud if you're on public transportation.

I keep a notebook (see "The Magic Notebook") for each writing project and an ongoing general writing journal. I use the notebooks for "writing through" plot problems, working out genealogies and time-lines, drawing maps and flow-charts. The journal's for cool names in search of characters, story ideas, that sort of thing. Sometimes, a half-hour spent noodling through the work in progress or dreaming about the next one can make the difference between a day of frustration and excuses and one that, while not enormously productive of written pages, supercharges me for weeks to come.

Notes

Interruptions

When I first started writing, way back in fourth grade, I worked on one story at a time. It never occurred to me that it was possible to have multiple writing projects in different stages. As I got older, the pile of stories begun and then abandoned grew. I noticed how rare it was for me to return to a story once I'd run out of steam. I either wrote it all the way through or it ended up on the Pile of Doom. Through high school and college (summers), I completed more of what I began. My gift to myself after graduating college was to write a novella, and after graduate school, I finished my first novel. (All of these were utterly unpublishable, but they had beginnings, middles, and most importantly, endings.) I was still at the stage of On/Off writing.

Shortly after my first child brought joy and unanticipated chaos to my life, my writing career shifted into a new gear, with both fanzine publications and my first professional short story sale. Over the next decade or so, I had to learn a new mode of writing: *On/Off/On/Off/On....* For one thing, I often had only very short periods of time in which to madly type out the scenes I had been rehearsing in my head. For another, I was writing both novels and short fiction. Sometimes I'd stick the shorter works in between drafts of the novels, which was helpful in terms of "clearing my head" so that I could return to the novel with fresh eyes. Sometimes I had a specific market and deadline for the short story and had to set aside the novel in whatever stage it was in. I would do just that, with no special preparation, and then re-read what I had written to "come up to speed." Most of the time, that would be sufficient to jog my memory about what I intended to come next. Occasionally I'd be left with the vague and disquieting feeling that I'd forgotten some brilliant plot twist or other element. Such are the risks of being a "pantser" (writing "by the seat of the pants") instead of using outlines.

Gradually I made more sales, novels as well as short stories, and improved my skill at alternating projects in different stages (Project 1 first draft, Project 2 outline, Project 1 revise, Project 2 first draft, rinse and repeat). I experimented with sequential leapfrogging and with handling different projects at different times of day (mornings for revision, afternoons for first drafts, or vice versa). So far, so good.

Then life handed me Interruptions. Non-negotiable Interruptions. The good ones involved having to drop whatever new project I was working on for reviewing copy edits, revising to editorial feedback, or proofreading a book in production. It simply isn't professional to tell your editor, "Yes, I know this book has a tight deadline, but I simply can't set aside this on-spec novella, so you'll simply have to wait until the muse takes a vacation."

Typically, these production schedule interruptions run from a few weeks to several months, depending on the publisher's schedule and the amount of work required. A few scribbled notes sufficed as memory aids for whatever work I was in the middle of. 2013 was different. Because I had four novels and a short story collection scheduled, I ended up with nonstop revision/copy-edit-review/proofreading for almost eight months. And I was in the middle of a new novel I was very excited about, one of those "attack novels" that just carries you along as it writes itself. A few notes wouldn't be enough to re-capture that momentum. So before I closed the folder for that book, I spent several days brainstorming and writing down every idea that excited me about where the plot should go, what crisis points the characters would face, and what emotional notes I wanted to hit. This wasn't the same as an outline because I wanted to keep as many options open as possible. I wanted a playing field rich in possibilities. If I'm working from an outline, I've already gone through the process of discovery, or a close enough approximation thereof so that I can trust what I have already created. This novel, unlike those I sell on proposal these days, did not have an outline. So when I return to it, I need that original exhilaration and fermentation of ideas more than I need "this comes next."

The second sort of involuntary interruption involves an inability to write. Not "writer's block" or, as Maya Kaathryn Bohnhoff put it, "writer's gap" (you know where you want to end up, you just have no clue as to how to get from here to there), but a crisis that brings all creative activity to a halt. It can be internal or external: depression, the death of a loved one, serious illness, trauma, natural disaster, criminal legal proceedings, child custody disputes, or anything that rocks us so deeply that the connection to our creative selves is fractured. This happened to me following the first parole hearing of the man who raped and murdered my mother. I went through a period of several years of not being able to write (or, for much of it, to read fiction); all my very tenuous focus went toward surviving from one day to the next. Every unfinished project stayed that way, and nothing new got started.

Eventually I recovered enough to look around at the shards of my career and start picking up what I could. I wrote some new stories, which helped me to rediscover the focus necessary to tackle a novel-length work again. I had a few projects "from before" in various stages of completion. One novel that was at submission level eventually sold (#2 out of 4 for 2013). Another I relegated to the trunk, on the advice of my agent, as too scattered and episodic to succeed. A couple of novelettes remain in their folders with a few "from before" rejection slips. I have no idea what to do with them. They have promise but serious flaws as well. I can't get my head back into the space in which I wrote them, and I don't think I want to.

The thing to remember is that when we return to projects suspended because of crisis, we do so *as different people*. Interruptions due to crash-and-burn deadlines may strengthen critical skills, but they don't generally cause us to reach deep into ourselves and emerge stronger but scarred. I'm not the writer or the person I was when I drafted those shorter pieces or that fractured novel. I've changed irrevocably and can never return. My life has been put back together in a different shape, with a different vision. Maybe at some time in the future, something in those stories may speak to me, but the solutions I come up with then will be very different from whatever I might have done "from before."

Sometimes interruptions are just that—a diaper that needs to be changed right now, a revision your editor wants next week. But sometimes they aren't so much interruptions as they are sideways quantum slips, leaving our lives and our work forever altered.

DEBORAH J. ROSS

Notes

When Writing Friends Aren't

Elsewhere on the net, a talented new writer made a comment about the damaging effects of another person's behavior. We can encounter destructive relationships in every area of our lives, but when it comes to our creativity, they can be particularly nasty.

Some people write in isolation. Either they aren't naturally sociable or they find that critical feedback simply isn't helpful. Most of us, however, create some type of support system at some stage of our careers. Often it's early on, when we're struggling to learn the craft. We may find a face-to-face group or an online workshop or other network of fellow novices. The Internet provides a wealth of opportunities to meet such people, as do conventions.

Most of the time, beginning writers are honestly trying to help one another. We may make mistakes as we learn how to give useful critical feedback or make idiotic suggestions about marketing, but the basic relationship is one of good will and support. Success, however small the sale, becomes an occasion for celebration. When one member improves, we all feel encouraged.

Trust is a crucial element in such groups. We work hard to learn to accept criticism, to not be defensive, to take time to think through the comments. While this vulnerability makes us more teachable, it also leaves us open to manipulation and abuse.

Sadly, sometimes the people we thought were our friends and supporters, our colleagues and conspirators in the adventure of creating and publishing stories, turn out to be our most insidious adversaries. Sometimes the alarm comes in the form of a sinking feeling, a sense that verges toward futility, after a discussion with a particular person. Other times, we realize that once again, we've been lured away from time in which we intended to work.

Often we have no idea how that happened. We want to think well of our friends; we believe their words even when their actions speak differently.

The whole issue of jealousy and sabotage on the part of those we have trusted with our creative process, those we have relied on to be both honest and tender with us, is complex and troubling. I can't do justice to all its aspects here. The first step toward healthier boundaries is realizing what is happening and that we are not alone. It's happened to most of us.

I don't mean to say that people join writer's workshops with the intention of eroding the self-confidence, not to mention the craft skills, of the other members. I do mean that people are not always aware of their own feelings and motivations. A person may truly believe he or she means nothing but the best for another writer, all the while subtly and unconsciously communicating something very different.

A writing friendship can begin as mutual support but not fare well when one writer's career takes off and the other one's doesn't. We're not supposed to feel jealous of another writer, especially a friend. But without self-awareness, it's easy to slide into resentment. ("It's not fair that he got published and I didn't when my story is just as good.")

Sometimes, resentment comes out in statements that undermine trust in the other writer's judgment and work, pressure to go against natural strengths, for example, to change genres or aim for unreasonable markets ("Why are you wasting your time writing sword and sorcery when you should be writing steampunk?")

Occasionally, envy will prompt a writer to try to manage the other's career, even to act as a sort of agent. Gossip is a common way of venting frustration, damaging both reputations and trust. ("She only got that story published because she slept with the editor.")

For me, it's important to find people I can trust, both within the field and outside it. Sometimes I need a disinterested listener, one I know will hold whatever I say in confidence, so I can work out what my guts are telling me and how to deal with the situation. This helps me to recognize my own "warning signs" and develop a vocabulary of responses. I also need regular time with fellow writers, not only to chew over specific writing problems but for general communication-of-enthusiasm and mutual cheering-on. When I do this regularly, I am less apt to be drawn into those relationships that are unhealthy for me as a person and as a writer.

Notes

Creative Jealousy

How many times have we heard someone say—or said ourselves—that we were jealous of a successful writer?

I have several problems with this. One is how destructive it is to our relationships, to our peace of mind, even to our creativity. It focuses our attention on something utterly beyond our control and puts enormous pressure on us to write for a certain result... instead of to write what is in our hearts, the very best and most authentic stories we can tell. By concentrating on another writer's success as an indication of our own failure, we are comparing their "outsides"—what the world thinks of them—with our "insides"—how we see ourselves. We will never know what it is like to be them inside, to struggle with their doubts, their disappointments and self-inflicted agonies. All we see is the face they show to the world, and by judging them on that basis, we risk losing compassion not only for them but for ourselves.

It helps me to think of envy rather than jealousy. Envy is wishing I were like another person, that I too might receive something another person has. Jealousy is wanting that thing *instead* of them. It's based on the notion of scarcity. In literary success, certainly, artificial measurements create and strengthen that illusion. After all, if the NYTimes Bestseller list consists of x books, that's all that will be included, regardless of quality. We get caught in the belief that there are only so many books that can be published and if someone else's book gets picked, then there's no room for ours. Ultimately, this may be true, but it's not helpful to us as individuals to see the pie as limited in size.

This is one area where the Internet is indeed changing the game. I think we're in a period of sorting-through wheat from chaff, that is, developing structures and processes to connect readers with the books they want to read. The old limitations of distribution and the budgets of publishers' sales departments no longer apply. An eternal optimist, I like to think that eventually the hype and the gaming-the-Internet will give way to new ways for readers to find well-written, rewarding stories.

Even if we restrict our consideration to print publication, I think it's much healthier to imagine the pie as expandable. On the scale of a single book sale or ten books or any number we ourselves are likely to be marketing at any one time, the more good books there are, the more we all benefit. I have found this attitude over and over again in the science fiction and fantasy community, where writers are enthusiastic readers and fans of one another's work. I also find that when I can shift my attitude just a little from "there are not enough publishing slots for everyone, so that person has taken mine" to "Wow, another great book for me to enjoy!" I am much more likely to step away from resentful comparisons and value my own work, my own creative voice.

One of the high points of my early literary career was meeting Poul Anderson at one of Marion Zimmer Bradley's "Fantasy Worlds" conventions. I found him standing alone at the reception for the guests and got up my nerve to introduce myself. He listened and then asked, with immense kindness and sincerity, "And what are you working on now?" He conveyed by tone and expression that he saw me not as a competitor but as a fellow writer of wonderful new stories for him to discover and enjoy. I want to be part of a community that offers that kind of support to one another — and it begins here, with me.

Notes

Encountering Wannabee Writers

Somewhere on the intarwebs, I read: "Authors Write Today; Pretenders Write Tomorrow." The implication is that if you are a *real* writer, you write all the time. Write as in, you deliver your thousand or five hundred or twenty-five hundred words, day in and day out. I think that's balderdash: it works for some writers, but not everyone. Some successful authors write in maniacal spurts, putting in 16-hour days, drafting novels in a few weeks, and then going long periods of time without any word output but with intense, deep rejuvenation and development of creative ideas.

The second, and perhaps more important aspect of the quote is the implication that being a "wannabee," a person who aspires to be a writer but never actually writes, is a bad thing. At best, a pathetic thing.

I am as likely as the next person to shower wannabees with advice on how to get started and stay motivated. I rarely pay attention to whether the advice is actually being solicited and whether it is helpful. I buy into the notion that this person should be other than the way he or she is, that wanting to write, dreaming about being a writer and talking endlessly about it, or pretending to be a writer, is unacceptable.

Sometimes, "wannabee" is a stage people pass through and either go forward to do the work of writing, or leave and go on to dream about something else. Other people stay with wanting/dreaming/talking. It seems to be sufficient for their emotional needs, and that means they're getting something of value from it. A sense of self-importance? Of belonging to the "cabal of writers?" Trying out daydreams of different possibilities? Getting attention from well-meaning, helpful authors?

I think there can be great value in daydreaming, even about things we will never do.

For most of my life, I've dreamt about being a ballerina. I had a few years of dance when I was a child, and then again as a young adult, but never the rigorous training necessary for professional performance (nor do I have a suitable body type for ballet). I think my life has been enriched by imagining myself dancing on stage, leaping and pirouetting to glorious music. It's a way of living a different life, seeing the world through the lens of a different art. I think the same might be true for people who want to write: what it's about is not necessarily wanting to actually spend endless hours learning the craft of handling prose, but imagining themselves as different people, of belonging to a different world, perhaps of escaping from the restrictions of the way their own lives have played out.

If there is value in dreaming and talking about wanting to write, I also wonder who it hurts? Does wanting take the place of actually doing it? (Some writers won't discuss their works-in-progress because doing so dissipates the build-up of creative energy.) Is that so bad a thing? Does imagining yourself a successful author drain off so much of your energy and ambition that keeps you in a dead-end job? If so, is the best way out of that situation to be shamed about never actually writing? Or does the aspiration provide a small but continuous impetus to change the situation?

I suspect that the worst thing about wannabees is that they are *annoying*. Their conversation has the superficial semblance of a writerly discussion without any substance. They dominate the conversation with their own story ideas (often in excruciating detail) and take up about as much of a professional writer's time as they can. I've been cornered by wannabees, politely listening and offering suggestions, only to realize that the point of the conversation was not a request for encouragement or tips on how to get started, but a captive audience for the wannabee's oration. The problem, as I see it now that I am calmer, is not that this person has never written a word, but that this person has presented one type of interaction under the guise of another. I've gotten myself trapped into being a captive listener (and one that conveys status because I am a Published Author) under false pretenses. So of course I'm irritated.

Most of us who have been around fans with poor social skills figure out how to gracefully detach ourselves from prolonged interactions. We learn how to be courteous while maintaining appropriate professional social boundaries. But because so many of us love talking about writing and have been encouraged by those writers who have gone before us, we are particularly vulnerable to the desire to "pay forward" to newer writers. We don't have an accurate perception of the "wannabee game," which is not about learning writing craft but sharing enthusiasm for a daydream.

Once we recognize that's what is going on, we can acknowledge the other person's aspirations without getting drawn into a tedious and frustrating attempt to teach someone whose goal is not to learn.

Notes

The Lady (Actual and Honorary) Writers' Lunch

Writing is a lonely business. Well, maybe if you write screenplays as part of a committee, it isn't, but for most of us, the process involves endless hours with just us and the words on the page. No wonder we end up talking to our characters and listening when they talk back. There's a listing for that in the DSM-IV.

One of my secret weapons against the perils of isolation is the writer's lunch. When I lived in Los Angeles, I joined my first critique group, an eclectic mix of science fiction and fantasy writers, mystery writers, and mainstream "literary" writers, with a core of Clarion and UCLA Advanced Writing class graduates. One of the other science fiction writers and I started going to lunch once a month or so. The group meetings were tightly focused on critiquing manuscripts and there wasn't much time for schmoozing about general writing issues, nor was the group atmosphere hospitable to science fiction shop talk. I quickly learned the value of having a writing buddy, someone to cheer me on, help me choose markets, analyze the personalities of editors, commiserate with about rejections (and try to interpret those letters), and more.

Kay Kenyon put it like this:

Don't make the mistake of thinking that to be a writer you mostly have to hunker down and write. You do, of course, have to write. But you also have to survive the slings and arrows of a very tough business. For this, there is nothing like a friend.

'If possible, a very close friend. A best pal can anchor you in the writing life, providing:

Advice and problem-solving.
A friendly ear when one hits bottom.
Someone who'll applaud you without (too much) envy when a success comes.
A companion for conferences and signings.
A mirror to your own writing life, to give perspective.
Source of laughs, gossip, and wisdom.
Dependable guerrilla marketing and cross-promotions with you.

My first writing buddy and I eventually went our separate ways, but by then I'd found other like-minded writers. A few of these were writers I admired tremendously and were much further along in their careers than I was. From them I learned new ways of looking at the business, and also that I'd been judging my own progress far too harshly. I learned that even successful authors have crises of confidence, think their work is dreadful but know how to revise like maniacs, get rejected, and get dropped by agents or publishers. And then they pick themselves up, switch genres, change names, and get right back into the game. So when some of those things happened to me, I knew I wasn't the only one and I knew it was possible to recover, reinvent myself, and go on.

After I moved to the redwoods, I did a lot less of this sort of networking. For one thing, there were far fewer writers in this rural area, although for a time I did attend a very small beginner's group, mostly to hear people talk about writing. I did a certain amount of schmoozing online, as time permitted, because I was now working full time as a single mom. Also, I was beginning the Darkover collaborations, and for various reasons it wasn't appropriate to workshop them. I missed that face-to-face camaraderie.

When attending Baycon, the closest regional science fiction and fantasy convention, I hooked up with a new writer friend. I loved what she had to say and we instantly hit it off. Both of us had the same sense of give-and-take, of listening and advising, of asking questions and sharing experience. Before long, we'd figured out a half-way point from our homes and set up a lunch date. So was born The Lady Writers' Lunch.

The name, Lady Writer's Lunch, is a play on the Lady Writer's Commune. Once when I was feeling discouraged and anxious about my financial future, a dear friend (also a writer) said, "If worst comes to worst, we can pool our Social Security checks, rent an old house in the country, and set up a little old lady writers' commune." I laughed so hard, I cried, and the image of writers supporting one another has stayed with me.

My new writing buddy and I wrestled through story planning, plot and character problems, getting an agent, pulling a project from a publisher, balancing writing in more than one genre, how to write with kids at home, how to write through tragedy, how to use social media and keep it from eating our lives. (We've found that IM can serve well for moment of support or just a "Hey, I've finished a scene!" "Hooray!") From time to time, we'd include others, and the group has gradually grown, averaging about four. Right now we've got a male writer, too. The joke is that we've made him an Honorary Lady.

One of the gifts of such a group is not the support I receive from it, but the honor and joy of watching someone else come into her own as an artist, to celebrate her achievements. It's the opposite of Schaudenfreude—it's taking immense pleasure and pride in the success of someone you have come to care about.

Notes

Mentoring

People ask me if Marion Zimmer Bradley was my mentor, or they simply assume she was. Mentoring is a term that's thrown around a lot these days, and I often wonder what it really means. So I looked up the definition and found:

1. a wise and trusted counselor or teacher;

2. an influential senior sponsor or supporter.

The definition gives me four essential qualifying relationships: counselor, teacher, sponsor, or supporter. That covers a whole lot of territory. Half the science fiction/fantasy community would go on my list, either as mentors or mentees. I need a narrower definition.

Its seems to me that mentoring, as the term is currently used, goes beyond "support" and instruction. It involves advising a younger writer and shaping that writer's career. This function was once served by editors and agents; in some cases, it still is. But most aspiring writers find themselves adrift in unknown territory, where the rules are nebulous and constantly changing, and every writing blog shrieks out advice.

We human beings need, if not security itself, then the illusion of it. *Someone's* got to know how it works, right? In terms of the writing itself, there are people who've figured out a thing or two. Some of them teach classes, and others will critique specific manuscripts. But publishing is changing so rapidly and in so many unanticipated directions that anyone who says they know the secret is selling you something. A newbie with good market instincts (c.f., Amanda Hocking) is as likely to meet with spectacular success as someone with forty hardcover novels in print. In other words, all bets are off when it comes to publishing "guidance."

What about mentoring, then? I think we need to soften—or broaden— the definition. The old model of wise-old-counselor-authority must give way to mutual sharing of experience and opinion in an environment of respect and encouragement. Which brings me back to Marion Zimmer Bradley. One of the most satisfying (if occasionally terrifying) aspects of our relationship was that from very early on, she treated me like a peer. Certainly, she had things to say about my writing when it was clumsy and ill-though-out. Rather emphatic things. But she never advised me about where to submit what or what I should be writing next, how to publicize my work, what conventions to go to, or whom to introduce myself to. She always talked to me as if I were a competent person, a writer with my own dreams and artistic vision who just happened to have fewer years of publishing than she did.

Over the years, I've had the privilege of extending the same respect to writers with less experience, just as Marion did to me. I meet regularly with a friend, an immensely talented writer near the beginning of her career. I love hearing about her current project and being able to vent about the frustrations in mine. Am I her mentor? Is she mine? Or are we each sharing our different strengths, our fears, our enthusiasm?

Marion was my friend, my editor, and my colleague. She encouraged me. She loved my work. I admired her tremendously and will always be grateful and honored by her confidence in me. Was she my mentor?

Does it matter?

Notes

Exercise for the Older Writer

It seems that the older I get, the more integral exercise is to my writing practice. The way they are interwoven has changed with the passing decades, as has the type of physical activity that appeals to me. I no longer exercise to change my appearance (not that this ever was a huge motivation, but I think all young people have some measure of physical vanity). I think more about staying healthy and maintaining the strength and flexibility that allow me to do *other* things I enjoy, like sitting comfortably while I write, exploring new places, and having adventures. First and foremost, however, I like to do things that are fun. So I'm not going to give you a litany of all the reasons you should exercise to prevent heart disease or stave off Alzheimer's. I'm going to talk about the ways being active have made me a better writer, in ways that I couldn't appreciate when I was a newbie.

Once upon a time, I was an active kid. I didn't think about exercise *per se*, I thought about *playing*. I ran through sprinklers, I rode my bike and attempted to roller-skate, I played outdoor games with my friends, but best of all, I acted out the stories I made up, either with my friends or by myself. I think this was my first and foundational experience of how glorious, how unexpected and consuming and enriching story-telling might be. As kids, we threw ourselves into one adventure after another. Granted, much of it was derivative, a sort of live-action fanfic. What we could do physically—climb trees, build snow forts, crawl under bushes, sneak around buildings—we did, and the rest we mimed as best we could. Stories were experienced not just with words, but with our whole bodies.

As readers, haven't we had the experience of feeling our heart rate accelerate and our muscles tense during a particularly suspenseful scene? Our visceral reactions mirror the action of the story, linking us to the characters and their plight. So many times, I've read a passage that skillfully depicts some action and thought, *I know what that feels like*. I'm in that character's shoes, or riding boots, or skin-diving flippers, or crampons, or toe shoes.

Speaking now as a writer, it's one thing to do my research and get the details of an activity right. It's another thing to have actually done it and to know what it feels like from the inside of my body, those kinesthetic and proprioceptive details that will draw the reader even further inside the scene. Joints flex, muscles strain under heavy weight, weight shifts, teeth slam together, ligaments stretch as they are strained, injuries swell and stiffen. We know the different qualities of pain, for instance: a burn does not feel like a broken blood vessel or a sprain or an abrasion or a puncture or the lactic-acid ache of exhaustion or the throb of a migraine.

It's unrealistic, not to mention foolhardy and actually impossible, to attempt to experience every action we give our characters to do. As much as I would like to, I will in all likelihood never go into space, and I'm not willing to go bungee-jumping off the Golden Gate Bridge. But the more things I have experienced, the more likely I'll be able to find an analogy to what I want to describe. Look at it this way: human bodies bend only so many ways, intact ones, that is. My hip and knee will flex deeply whether I'm rock climbing or using a stirrup to mount a tall horse or clambering up a set of stairs created by alien giants. I have a sense of how I have to shift my weight over the top foot, or take a hop off my standing leg. I also know that my knees don't feel exactly the same when they're bent that far, and I've got a hitch in one hip at the extreme range of motion.

As I've gotten older, two truths have emerged. One, I don't have to do it all. I don't have the time, and I've come to terms with the fact that there are some things I am never going to be able to accomplish: become a professional opera singer or an Olympic gymnast, for example. Two, I don't have to do it all, but it will make my writing as well as my life richer if I keep learning, keep stretching, keep challenging myself physically in appropriate ways. Those ways have changed. When I was a child and then a young adult, I had many more possibilities and far fewer physical limits than I have now. My body requires more care to remain strong and flexible, but my imagination requires even more. It needs not only intellectual stimulation, but new and renewed ways of interacting with the physical world through my body.

Notes

Listening

Whenever I hear of a friend or relative—or a stranger, I'm not picky!—in distress, I want to jump in and fix their lives. It's so much easier dealing with someone else's problems than my own. Besides, I am at times the world's authority on everything (things and times being variable). So I do my best to keep my mouth shut.

I'm long since realized what a disservice I do to those I care about by butting in with unasked-for advice. It doesn't matter whether my perspective is correct and my facts accurate, or that what I suggest would work a whole lot better than what they're doing. What matters is that these are my facts and my solutions, and I have usurped the resourcefulness of the other person and denied them the dignity of finding their own way through a problem.

Not only that, and more importantly, I haven't *listened*. By filling my mind with problem-solving instead of attending to experience and emotion, I've cheated myself out of a priceless opportunity to glimpse life through someone else's eyes. I've also deprived them of perhaps the most precious gift a friend can offer, a compassionate and undemanding ear.

Some time ago, a writer friend who was going through a difficult divorce told me that her therapist had been amazed at her ability to understand and empathize with her spouse's point of view. She was puzzled by this response. As writers, we cultivate our creative imagination, the insight that gives us a window into characters very unlike ourselves. While I'm not suggesting that things told to us in confidence should be fodder for the creative grist mills, I do believe that careful listening, deep listening, can make us better writers as well as better friends.

DEBORAH J. ROSS

Notes

When Is It Enough?

One of the challenges in growing older is having to adjust the amount of food I eat. Like many women, I've battled with my weight for my entire adult life, and have kept it mostly under control with careful food selection and regular exercise. I had reached an understanding with my appetite, a truce of sorts, and maintained a fair degree of equilibrium. Then menopause hit, and a decade later, it is finally penetrating my brain that I cannot eat as much as I used to without gaining weight (which, now for health reasons rather than vanity, is not desirable). In other words, I no longer know how much is enough.

I fought this realization for years. I clung to the illusion of being able to navigate three meals a day, whether at home or in a convention hotel restaurant, without having to think too much. Now I have gotten as far as making my peace with re-defining "enough food," although I don't always know what that new amount is.

It strikes me that there is a parallel process in learning to write. When we begin, we have no idea how much is enough—enough description, enough dialog, enough scenes, enough blows in the blow-by-blow sequences. What's too little? What's too much? It takes experience and critical reflection to judge. My own version was that I'd either write stories that were so minimalist, the most important story elements verged on becoming non-existent, or else I'd belabor every detail, no matter how trivial.

I'd think that because I had worked hard to craft a single sentence (or even a phrase), it would necessarily carry a similar weight with the reader. Surely, those few words would convey the full impact of all that travail. Surely, the reader would fill in all the carefully-understated gaps, would realize every nuance and spot every subtlety. While I still believe in giving the reader credit for being intelligent, I've come to understand that the material has to be on the page to begin with. Even perceptive, literate readers aren't telepathic. We have to give them a clue here and there, more here than there if it's something important.

I also fell prey to the widespread beginner's error that the amount of text on the page (and hence, the time it takes to read it) ought to correspond to the speed of the action itself. Fast action's a short scene, right? The truth is that the more dramatic a scene is, the more "weight" of detail it can support. An essential element in suspense is "playing the scene out." Overdone brevity undercuts the build-up of tension and deprives the reader of that very experience she expects from the story.

At the same time, I'd excessively elaborate details without reference to their importance. (Actually, the word "excessively" points out that even crucial details can be overstated.) Some of my tools-in-crime were exaggeration, inappropriate diction, and repetition. I described every object, every character, every bit of action, with multiple adjectives, and I couldn't use a simple verb like, "said" or "ran" or "was." I twisted sentences into excruciating shapes in my efforts to avoid the verb "to be." I thought the more syllables an adverb had, the more it added to the color of the sentence.

What, isn't the "purple" in "purple prose" a strong color-word and a good thing? And my goodness, I can't risk the reader not getting *this* point! So I'd better highlight it every time it comes up, just in case they missed it the first time.

In my early years, I focused on cutting out the redundancies and overwritten prose. I learned to "flesh out" my scenes, to draw out moments of drama, to slow down the action, and to give the reader time to savor whatever is going on. As I've gotten more skillful, I've learned to do it more with fewer words. I've found different ways of "playing things out," of creating resonances instead of inflicting repetitions on the reader. I strive to evoke rather than delineate. I try to make every story element serve multiple purposes (for instance, advancing the plot *and* revealing character *and* adding backstory, or setting the scene *and* heightening tension *and* suggesting the larger world).

What is enough has, like the food on my plate, gotten smaller. What is too much, on the other hand, requires never-ending vigilance.

Notes

Nourishing Yourself

Surviving as a Writer (or Artist… or Musician)

There's no dearth of articles on strategies for financial survival. The Internet abounds in them, some excellent, but many more that seem to be unfounded blatherings. At a time when publishing is changing faster than news can spread, a person can say just about anything and be right some of the time. This isn't one of those. This is about surviving psychologically.

The two sorts of survival are connected. Struggling financially, being unable to support yourself with your writing (insert as appropriate: art, dance, music, etc.) is frustrating and discouraging. I think it's even more so when reaching that readership, that group of people who love your work and for whom your work has enduring value, is part and parcel of the rewards of being a writer. I also think that each one of us forges our own way through the thorn-forest of publishing/getting paid/writing/dreaming. Here are a few things that work for me. They might be helpful to you, too.

If the only thing I loved about writing was getting paid for it, I'd probably give up and go back into health care. If I either hated or was indifferent to the writing itself, it simply wouldn't be worth the hassle. At least, helping sick people get better comes with warm fuzzy feelings and a regular paycheck. I'm fortunate in that writing fiction isn't the only thing I can do for that paycheck. Don't get me wrong, it's wonderful to get paid. It just isn't sufficient in itself for me.

What if I knew no one would ever read what I wrote? That's stickier. I began writing, somewhere around 4th grade, without any intention of reaching an audience (well, beyond my parents, who enthused over every effort). As a teen, I sent a few stories out without any idea of what I was doing. By the time I started submitting seriously, I'd started about a gazillion novels and finished a few of them, as well as many more short pieces. All for what? For the pleasure in telling the story.

I come back to that principle again and again, in many variations. I don't see any point in slogging through a story that's drudgery to write (and will therefore be boring to read). Scenes can be difficult or painful to write. They can challenge me in terms of skill or raw emotional honesty. So *pleasure* in the sense of *ease* is misleading. Perhaps a better way to express this is the sense that this is worth doing, and worth doing right. We know that kids love mastering new skills and learning new information. Tackling a difficult story element—a scene, a point of view, some technical aspect that presents a high-wire act—may be excruciating at the same time as it is exhilarating.

So I write in part for the satisfaction of telling a story and telling it well. I write stories I myself want to read. But there came a time in my development as a writer when I wanted to share those stories with other people. Herein lies the challenge: what role does the completion of communication play in how I feel about writing? Is it enough to run off copies (or send files) to my family and close friends? Once upon a time, there weren't a lot of choices besides traditional publishers if I wanted to reach a wider audience. Publishers act as gatekeepers in the worst sense and as guarantors of editorial quality in the best. If I let my publisher (or editor, or agent) be the sole arbiter of my work, I may be enlisting an invaluable ally in both commercial success and in determining the worth of my work. But that's a two-edged sword, as too many have found to their sorrow.

The question for those being published in traditional ways is, *How do I remain true to my internal compass and stay receptive to that advice which is valuable to me?* What happens when sales figures over which I have no control result in rejection (declining advances being yet another aspect of this). How do I find satisfaction in the work itself, regardless of what's happening in New York or amazon.com?

If I go the self-publishing route, all too easy these days, must I sacrifice the mentor/teacher/gadfly role of a professional editor? How do I keep growing as a writer, keep learning new stuff and practicing what I know to make it seem effortless? How do I stay humble in my art? Or is that important to me? Maybe it's pretentious or destructive to think in those terms. Or maybe it's essential.

The real gift of all the venues offered by the Internet is that they allow me to separate publication anxiety from the joy of storytelling. If all I want is to get the words down, they can stay on my computer. If what I want is to throw them out and say, *I had a whale of a good time writing this and I think you might enjoy reading it, for fun and for free*, I can put it up on my website or other places on the 'net. If I believe the story has merit and for whatever reason does not suit traditional publishers, I can do what many (some say, far too many) have done and make it available for money. The point is that I no longer have to feel locked in to evaluating my work by the commercial marketing decisions of a corporate publisher.

Sure, I can put up drek. But I can also use that same freedom to keep my focus on writing the stories that are wonderful to me, to the best of my ability. That is what has kept me writing all these years, and that is the only thing I know that will for sure continue to do so.

Notes

Defining Writing Success as Publishing

Some writers, and successful professional writers at that, began as daydreamers with no thought of becoming published. Whether they wrote fanfic or invented their own worlds, they went through a long period of writing just for themselves. I want to cry when I think of some of the wonderful writers who had to *hide* their work because of parental disapproval or employer requirements or other reasons. I think that's one reason I'm so encouraging of people in those early stages... you never know where those early Mary/Gary Sue stories might lead.

Other people knew early on that they wanted to be published. I don't know if there's a correlation between this goal-setting and preference for working on invitation and under contract (versus "on spec," where you don't know if there's a market for what you're working on, you just fly with it anyway). On the one hand, having such a goal can focus our efforts, perhaps boot us into serious critique groups, workshops, and classes earlier than we might if left to our own inclinations, because we're going about learning to write in a professional manner. That's a thought—being a professional writer even before we've sold anything, measured by *how we go about learning to write*.

The down side is that (until the Internet made self-publishing so easy) defining ourselves as writers by whether we are published relies on something beyond our control. Are we then setting ourselves up to feel like failures if the market does not cooperate with our timetable? Or does it serve us to have an objective measurement of the quality of our work so that we are held to higher standards, so we don't have the option of saying we don't care, what do editors know, they're all against us... the usual whiny excuses. It's a bit like weight lifting. The numbers don't lie.

One form of "numbers" is the value the marketplace assigns to our work. In the past, it's been the size of an advance, and to a lesser extent the prestige of the market. Add to that the sales figures, assuming we can decipher those amazingly baroque royalty statements. Self-publishing adds both positive and negative aspects. There's no longer a gatekeeper editor/publisher to say, "This book is worth this much in sales." We can prove them wrong… and know we're doing it. We can have direct access to our own sales figures. So, quality aside, we can define success as so many copies actually sold (not what the publisher thinks will sell).

If the (or one) source of pleasure and satisfaction in writing is doing it well, does it do us a disservice to set our goals by copies sold? This assumes we aren't one the edge of homelessness and financial considerations trump everything else, just looking at how we maximize the joy and sense of achievement from our work. If we take editorial feedback out of the equation, how do we measure our growth as writers? Professional reviews, growing fewer all the time? Reader reviews, which can be meaningless? Critique groups? Trusted beta readers? Book doctors?

Some experienced writers seem to have a strong inner critical sense, an ability to evaluate their own work by their own standards. It's a little like coming full circle from when we wrote only to please ourselves, only having slogged through the threshold criteria of professional publication. As I've grown as a writer, there have been more times when I know I've produced something good, but I always have blind spots. I get enamored of the most awful drek because I see what I *intended*, not what actually ends up on the page. Turning out flawed drafts does not mean I'm a poor writer… but *leaving* the work that way is a sure ticket to never improving!

Notes

Would You Write Anyway?

I've heard various versions of the question of whether you would continue to write if you knew absolutely-for-sure that your work would never be published. Self-publishing has made the question irrelevant. It's far easier to put together an ebook, a website, a blog, than it is to write a book in the first place.

The question is worth consideration, nonetheless, because it gets at some fundamental issues. For whom are we writing? How important is it to be told how wonderful our work is? Are we writing because we love storytelling or because we have a message we want to communicate (in which case, an audience is essential to our feeling of satisfaction)? Is our writing a way of generating income? (Don't scoff; I've met middling-successful writers who admit as much.)

I derive a great deal of pleasure when I know what I've just written is good (that thrill of reading it over and going, *OMG I wrote this and it's wonderful!*) and sometimes I don't care whether anyone else thinks so. It's enough that I'm pleased with what I've produced. But I would not be able to write as well as I sometimes can if I had not had critical feedback from others—lots and lots of it over the years. These others have been editors, fans, fellow workshoppers, trusted readers, other writers, reviewers whom I've never met but nonetheless offered insightful and sometimes extremely painful commentary. I owe them all more than I can say. I haven't written in a vacuum.

Mostly, I love feedback, or rather, I love most feedback. We'll forget the idiot reviews by people who obviously have not even read the book. Or who have some other axe to grind, but that's another topic. The short version is, if the material (usually but not always related to queer issues) irritates you, don't blame the quality of the writing. Tackle your demons head-on.

I've gotten fan letters that bring tears to my eyes, to know that my work has touched them that deeply and made such a difference in their lives. Reaching so many readers, people I'd never have the chance to meet in person, is one of the special gifts of being published.

If you were to ask me if I'd keep writing *now* if all my work would stay in a drawer, the answer would be yes. It doesn't have to be the case for everyone. I'm just one of those writers who finds the act of creation, both the exercise of hard-won skill and the stories themselves, so deeply satisfying that I'm willing to keep doing it even without the joys of connecting to readers (not to mention seeing my name in print and holding a book, thinking *I wrote this!*)

Notes

Zen Yoga Writing Practice

A confession: I like to read at bedtime. All the sleep hygiene experts say not to, that beds should be used only for sleeping and one other activity. What do they know? I find something deeply comforting about curling up with a good—but not too exciting—book. Perhaps it evokes memories of my mother reading aloud to me, or it's just "me time."

A few years ago, I started including in my nightly reading a page or two of something that stretches my mind. I don't mean that in the intellectual sense, for I definitely want to be quieting my thoughts, not forcing myself to think critically. I choose books that get inside my brains and stretch them gently in unexpected directions, like mental yoga before settling into my comfort reading.

I love Natalie Goldberg's *Long Quiet Highway*. Goldberg is a writing teacher, essayist, and novelist who is also a long-time student of Zen Buddhism. I was introduced to her work years ago with her *Writing Down The Bones*, and had always thought of her as a teacher in the style of Julia Cameron: "Morning pages," keep the pen moving, let your thoughts flow, that sort of advice. *Long Quiet Highway* is autobiographical rather than instructive. I was deeply moved by how she put together mundane, specific details in ways that brought tears to my eyes. More than that, she got me thinking—or rather, feeling/sensing—more deeply about the role of writing in my own life. Yes, it's a pleasure and an obsession; yes, it's my occupation, how I earn my living.

Mountain Pose: Could it also be the lens through which I view the world? Sure, no problem; every new experience is grist for the mill. That's the easy answer, just as the plot skeleton is the easy description of a story. As a writer, I know that storyness is much deeper than plot. Can I use that same insight to listen more deeply, look beyond appearances, appreciate the interwoven complexity of my community and environment?

Dancing Shiva Pose: How about writing as a spiritual practice? Um, isn't that a bit pretentious... or is it? Is there something moving through me, speaking through me, when I write from my heart? Can I shove my ego as well as my intellect out of the way? Speaking of intellect, and ego, and mind...

Pigeon Pose: Could writing help me become better acquainted with my own mind? The way my thoughts sometimes behave like grasshoppers on steroids? The phrases and connections and story elements I use repeatedly, without intention? The cycles of feeling I've written something fabulous, only to plummet to the certainty it's all drek, that I can never get anything right?

Corpse Pose: Is writing a way of stilling my thoughts and becoming fully present—through *words*, are you kidding? Ah, those moments when it feels like I'm not making up these words, they're coming from somewhere else, I'm just a lens, a focal point through which light passes.

I have no easy answers, but I will be watching myself—my self—more closely as I write. And who knows, I might even achieve a new literary Downward-Facing Dog.

Notes

Nothing Creative is Ever Wasted

Marion Zimmer Bradley used to say that the first million words were practice. It's both a daunting prospect and a relief. *Daunting:* You mean I have to write *ten* 100,000 word books before I get anything right? *A relief:* I have lots and lots of time in which to develop as an author. So what do we do with those ten books (or those hundred 10K short stories)?

Occasionally we prevail over the proclamation and we get it right. We sell a story and see it in print. Every blue moon it's someone's *first* story. OMG, as my kids would say. I don't know about how your mind works, but I immediately start expecting the same from myself. I forget that a *career* entails slow, steady improvement in skill, the gradual accumulation of experience, and lots of mistakes. If I'm not getting rejection letters, I'm not taking the risks I need to become better.

At any rate, by the time I sold my first novel, I'd accumulated a trunk full of writing—novels, shorts, fragments. Most of them were unsalable, not just because of the amateurish caliber of the prose but because the ideas themselves were "half-baked," poorly conceived and developed. As I learned to revise, I was able to take some of these stories, excavate the heart of them—whatever originally turned me on about them—and completely or substantially rewrite them. (*Northlight* was an example.) By far the larger portion remain relegated to that trunk.

This is important, as important as it is to not sit around doing nothing while waiting to hear back from an editor. (You should be hard at work on your next book!) The stories stayed in the trunk because by the time I had the critical skills to see what was wrong with them, my creative skills had grown as well. The new story ideas, plots, landscapes, and characters I was coming up with were far and away better than what I'd done even a year ago. I chalked the old ones up as Marion's practice wordage and moved on to something that was the best I could do *now*.

I've seen writers cling to that first unsold (and unsellable) novel, pouring all their time and energy into sequel after sequel. I also know writers who began with multi-volume series that were too complex and demanding for their skill level, and then set them aside to hone their writing craft on more skill-appropriate projects.

So what's this about nothing creative being wasted? First of all, there's Marion's practice principle. Then there are stories that you're not ready to write yet but they're grand and nifty stories, worth coming back to. Then there are stories that are never going to work, but have bits and pieces that still speak to you. I think of them as a sort of pirate's chest, a jumble of plastic beads and fake rubies, Spanish doubloons and splinters of Ygddrasil. I'll rifle through the chest, setting aside the things with rhinestones, looking for flakes of true gold. I'll strip away the settings of plastic and tin and hold in my hands a tiny seed. Sometimes it's not ready to sprout, but sometimes it's exactly what I need to plant in the carefully tilled loam that is my writing career today.

Notes

'Tis the Season to Get Crazy

The winter holiday season seems to be an engraved invitation to depression and desperation, all under the guise of jollity, and we writers are far from immune.

First of all, it's winter. Anyone with even a hint of a whisper of SAD (Seasonal Affective Disorder) has been feeling progressively more "blue" as the length and brightness of daylight wanes. In most parts of the US and Europe, it's cold. It's damp. It's gray. Too often, you're stuck inside so you're not getting as much exercise as you would in a milder season. True, there are benefits to being cooped up with nothing better to do than to pour yourself into the novel-in-progress. However, more times than not, you're stuck inside with piles of indigestible food and intoxicating drink, neither of which are conducive to good writing. (For those of us who are not Hemingway, anyway, and even then you could argue, as Damon Knight did, that alcohol never improved anyone's writing.)

Second of all, winter is apt to be a lean season, financially speaking, for writers. It's a long time between royalty checks and editors take vacations just like everyone else. This occurs at the same time as the annual frenzy of exhortations to buy-buy-BUY, as if love for someone must be measured by the price of gifts. For too many of us, the combination of gloom and slowdown and expectation of spending is more than enough to plummet us into feelings of inadequacy and paralysis. (Not to mention fears of becoming a bag lady or gent within the next two weeks.)

For those of us whose families did not support or approve of our writing, the holidays amount to putting fertilizer on those struggles. It's painful to face yet another family gathering in which the inevitable question is when are we going to get a "real" job, or the studied ignoring of our deepest dreams. I don't mean to say that the winter holidays do not enrich our lives with time spent with loved ones, and a spirit of goodwill and renewal. I love lighting candles in the long dark nights; I love singing songs, even those belonging to other faiths. I was fortunate to have a supportive family (and children who are proud of my literary achievements). But I also know far too many fine writers who don't get that acknowledgment.

This season, let's band together to counter the gloomies and the naysayers. If you know a writer who's having a hard time, pick up the phone or send a note of encouragement. Leave a supportive message on their Facebook page. If you're local, suggest a time-out from the holiday madness for writerly shop-talk over a cup of tea. Send virtual flowers—or real ones, if any grow in your garden at this season. If your gift-giving includes the spending of money, consider the newest book from your favorite author, a magazine subscription, an audiobook or ebook, a membership to a local con. Don't forget the things that only we writers can offer: how about the gift of Tuckerizing a friend's favorite pet in your next story? Or a certificate for reading aloud (funny voices optional) from your own work? Or use your networking savvy to get a book plate autographed by the recipient's favorite writer?

However your holidays unfold, remember to be kind to one another. The sun will return. I promise.

Notes

Pacing...

No, not walking back and forth in an agitated manner...

Not controlling the speed of action and rise of tension in your story...

The insight that came to me over morning oatmeal had to do with pacing *myself*. That is, balancing the outflow of words (ideas, scenes...) and "refilling the well."

When I first struggled to write at a professional level, I had a small child (as in 9 months). (For those of you without children, this usually means no time for sleep, let alone writing.) I learned to use very small amounts of time and to do a lot of "pre-writing," that is, mapping out the scene I was working on, rehearsing every detail in my mind, questioning whether what I imagined was really the best it could be and worked with the rest of the story, that sort of thing, so that when I finally got that precious 15 minutes or half an hour to sit down at the typewriter, I'd go like mad. I used to joke that I couldn't afford writer's block; the truth is that I'd already written the next few pages. All I had to do was transcribe them.

Now that baby and the next one are all grown up (and wonderful young women they are, too) and my days are largely unstructured. The challenge then becomes how do I keep those ideas flowing at a pace that matches what I can put on paper (or in phosphors). I'm learning to tell when I've done enough by internal signals (*"Rest, go do something else,"* urges my back-brain), rather than when I've run out of time. Very often, I'll get started on some other activity (making dinner, walking the dog, housework, yoga practice) and more ideas will pop into my head. I'm still of two minds as to whether it's better to drop what I'm doing (unhappy doggie notwithstanding) and get back to work or to simply let the "idea-well" fill again.

Notes

Community and Solitude

Recently, a couple of things got me thinking about this delicate balance between my need for deep inner-silence/listening-silence, uninterrupted focused writing time, playing-with-others, and the nourishment of a larger community. I think that most of us move back and forth along a continuum of how much alone time versus with-others time we need. Of course, some people are temperamentally more social than others; some of us move through our days and lives with more outward energy than others.

For writers, the balancing act poses special challenges. We spend so much of our working time interacting only with the story inside our heads and whatever medium we're using to get the words out. This isn't reflective, listening-silence time, but it is alone time. So when we emerge from a work session, particularly a long, emotionally draining session, we tend to grab for either frantically-social time (making up time with spouse or kids included) or else dodo-brain escape time (in which who knows or cares if there are other people around, we're in spin-down zone-out mode).

It's as if we've drained one particular creative energy tank so dry that we're utterly unbalanced. I get the image of a donkey laden with two water barrels, listing far to one side and wandering off the track. It's hard enough under normal circumstances to pause and ask what we really need, what our inner selves thirst for. When we're in that peculiar state of being wrought-up and wrung-out, it's even harder.

I do better when I pay attention to what nourishes me, especially those parts of me, those areas of my life, that get put on hold all too often. I need to —I love to write!—but I also need time to get quiet inside. Time to listen deeply to Spirit, inner and outer. And I do even better when some of this time is in community.

I also need time in which I feel connected to others. To my immediate family, to my dear friends, to my colleagues, to kindred-spirits. I need face-to-face time. I need touch. I need to feel a part of a greater whole, and that I and we are making the world a better place. If I spend all my time here, I end up feeling just as drained as if I spent none. The trick is keeping it all in fluid balance.

Notes

Cross Training for Writers

Many times over the years, I have been impressed with the "other" talents of writers I admire. We are not only novelists and crafters of short fiction, we are dancers, singers, teachers, composers, musicians, farmers, cake decorators, painters, martial artists, animal trainers, and athletes. One shared characteristic of these activities is that they are all forms of creativity. Not only that, they force us to use our minds (and our bodies) in different ways than writing does.

Writing is hard work and it's easy to get burned out. When we're tired and our minds have gone numb, we're tempted to think the remedy is to "zone out." Passive activities (like watching television) create the illusion of rest and refreshment, but all too often leave us feeling even more drained than before. I propose that what benefits us most is not "down" time but "differently-creative" time.

Years ago, I noticed that at the end of my day-job week, all I wanted to do was curl up, usually in front of television. However, if I could get myself to go dancing or to a concert, or even dinner with friends, I would finish the evening energized and enthusiastic about diving back into my current story the next morning. It was as if I'd started the weekend a day early, instead of dragging myself out of bed midway through Saturday and picking listlessly at last week's tepid efforts. I think the same process holds true regardless of whether or not we work a 9-to-5 day job.

Some years ago, I decided to treat myself to piano lessons. I'd never studied music before, although I'd sat through hundreds of hours of my daughters' lessons. Since I'm a skilled typist, I figured that the piano fingering would be simple. (I pause here for anyone who's played a keyboard instrument to snort incredulously in my general direction.) Needless to say, I was soon juggling trying to make my hands, wrists, and shoulders do something new and exciting, and also to wrap my mind around and through the internal structure of classical music, and also to listen to what I was playing. As frustrating as this process can be, it was also exhilarating. I was asking my brain—motor, sensory, cognitive and kinesthetic functions—to work in a new way, a new and creative way.

(I'm going to sidestep the issue of whether a musical performer is "creative" in the sense of adding anything to the composition. I will say instead that playing music is inherently creative because you've gone from silence to the active presence of an art form whose medium is sound. A dancer who is performing choreography is creative in the same way.)

An essential part of the care of a writer is "filling the well" or "recharging the batteries." It's rare to be able to pour forth volume after volume of peerless storytelling while sitting in a room by yourself, isolated and absorbed only in the work. Most of us need to actively engage with other people and in other activities, to rest one part of our minds while flexing and strengthening others, to stockpile a treasure trove of sights, sounds, dreams, thoughts, emotions, relationships. Acquiring a new skill—whether it's karaoke singing or mountain climbing, a Chopin *Prelude* or a perfect pirouette (human or equine), is a good way to begin.

Notes

On Writing and Healing

Some years back, my sister gave me a copy of Louise DeSalvo's *Writing as a Way of Healing* (Beacon Press, 1999). It sat on my shelf as I debated whether its contents would be grim or admonishing. I was wrong on both counts. Although my fiction writing is just that—fiction, as in "I made it all up, I truly did"—the book presented me with two invaluable gifts.

The first is that when we tell the truth, we improve not only our emotional but our physical health, and there's research to prove it. DeSalvo writes specifically about autobiographical narrative of trauma or other difficult situations. I think the same holds true in a broader sense for all writing. It does not matter that my character is not me or these things never happened in my own life. I can still tell the truth, the truth of my heart, the truth of my spirit. When I do that, something unfolds within me and is given space to breathe, to stretch, to grow into a different shape.

My Darkover novel, *Hastur Lord*, alternates points of view between a bisexual man in a love triangle and that of his gay male lover. I am not a man of any sexual orientation. Yet as I dug into myself to write about jealousy and inclusivity, the courage to face one's fears and the generosity to transcend them, the needs we can set aside and the needs that, if denied, can kill us, I found resonances within my own life. I remembered times when I acted badly and hurt the ones I love, and times I could not ask for what I needed because I didn't even know what that was. Did I make my characters speak for me? I hope not. Did they think and feel and act in ways that invited me to be more gentle with my own past? Absolutely.

The second gift of this book was DeSalvo's approach to writing as work. Commercial genre writing tends to encourage a regimental approach: you sit down, you pound out so many words or so many pages, you vent about this problem or that, you feel satisfied or not, depending on whether you achieved your daily quota. DeSalvo, on the other hand, encourages the writer to *prepare* for the day's work, just as an athlete or actor would prepare, and to *reflect* on the experience afterwards. This means getting friendly with our goals, our intuition, and our inner processes. When we hold in mind what we intend in whatever terms are meaningful for that particular day, we are ready to begin. Afterwards, we conclude—giving each session a beginning, middle and end, just like a good story. We deepen our understanding of what works best for us.

I love what she says about book-length works:

Writing longer works helps us mature. We learn persistence. We recognize that profound understanding takes time. In elaborating our first impressions, we discover there's more to our stories than we'd thought. We identify patterns in how we work, in our work, and in our lives.

All this takes time, which is important. As Isabel Allende observed in an interview... "You need a lot of time to exorcise the demons and take enough distance to be able to write with ambiguity and irony—two elements that are very important in literature."

She also points out, "Every published writer was once a beginner. Even seasoned writers, facing a new project, must start anew, begin anew."

Faced with a blank screen and an even more blank mind, I find this immensely reassuring.

Notes

Writing Fears

Tonight I had a brief conversation with a friend, touching on the social pressure to participate in an activity she found overwhelmingly frightening. This has got me thinking not only about what are my own "hot button" fears in general, but in my writing. We all have our individual crazy places, things about which we are not rational, things that create instant, flip-out, certifiably-nuts adrenalin overload. I've made my peace with how difficult some issues are for me. Over the years, with a lot of help from my friends, most of these have loosened their hold on me, even if they haven't entirely let go. I've come to believe that "courage is fear that has said its prayers," and know myself capable of a great deal despite those fears.

But what about writing? This is the new part. Are there things about writing in general, publishing, career, my own work, that intimidate me? Are there things I do or don't do because of fear? A few obvious fears I can cross off my list. I'm not afraid:

Of having a book or a story rejected.

Of receiving a harsh review.

Of making a fool of myself on a convention panel.

Been there, done that, got the T-shirt. None of these things is any fun at all, but being embarrassed isn't fatal, and a sense of humor will go a long way. One reason I love networking with other writers is that we aren't all off-balance on the same day. We've all been through some version of the above, and someone is sure to say exactly the right thing to carry me through the worst. Then I get to do the same for another friend.

I have moments of self-doubt, in which my thoughts go in unfortunate directions, prompting me to believe, if only for a moment, that nothing I've written is any good, I can't write my way out of a wet paper bag, and no one will ever want to read my work again. Fortunately, these moments are so brief and so easily made ridiculous, I don't categorize them as fears.

However, I am afraid:

Of letting myself get talked into wasting precious years on a project that's not meaningful to me.

Of not having the courage to tackle painful or controversial material.

Of dying before I tell the stories in my heart.

This kind of pressure—*I Must Write Stories Of Earth-Shaking Significance*—is not helpful. Who is to say what work will be cherished a century hence? Perhaps it won't be that Momentous Tome, but a bit of fluff—air and eathers and sheer delight. This is what fear does to us, thought, it makes us all tight. Desperate. Grim.

Talk about dying? Better, talk about living, about falling in love with every story, even the most fanciful. About letting that love, that joy, shine through. These things are, after all, ephemeral, but the memory of having experienced them is not.

After all, today is all any of us have. This present moment. This present story. This scene. This word. This unfolding of the heart.

Notes

Goals vs. Wishes

Quite some time ago, in the late 1970s I think, I stopped making New Year's resolutions (which always seemed to me to be engraved invitations to guilt) and started making goals. One-year, five-year, ten-year, and lifetime goals. They'd be something like:

1 year—write three short stories
5 years—sell a story
10 years—sell a novel
Lifetime—win a major award

As years rolled by, I wrote those stories, and I sold one and then another, and the goals shifted. Sometimes they got more specific, like "one year—finish X project" and sometimes more vague, "Write a work of enduring literary quality." Items came and went, like getting an advance of Y dollars or getting published in hard cover or getting reviewed in Z publication. I found that the more I achieved, the less satisfied I was with how I was progressing with my goals.

Why? I was working well and selling my short stories and novels regularly. I loved my work. But I was confusing *goals* with *wishes*. A goal is something I can achieve by my own effort. *My goal is to finish Chapter 27; my goal is to hike 5 miles; my goal is to play the Brahms Waltz in A Flat.*

A wish can seem like a goal—it's something I want and have to work for. But its achievement relies on some aspect that is beyond my control. I can *want* to win a Pulitzer Prize, I can *work* my brains out to that end, but I can't control the factors that lead to such recognition. As I gained more professional experience, I became more realistic in what I could and couldn't control. One novel sale does not guarantee the next. I have absolutely no way of making a movie studio take enough interest in my book to option its film rights. I can't force my publisher not to lay off my editor if that's what they must do (this has actually never happened to me, but it has to my friends).

So some things become wishes. *I wish that my book be selected by the Science Fiction Book Club. I wish that it sell overseas. I wish I get invited to be Guest of Honor at my favorite convention.*

With time comes wisdom.

I wish that my words bring hope and comfort to those in hard times.

I wish that my stories help to further understanding and acceptance of all peoples.

I wish that my heart may speak through my work.

Notes

Settling in Meditation and in Writing

Quakers call it "centering down," but I like the word, "settling." It reminds me of settlers, pioneers and voyageurs who have, for some utterly unaccountable reason, taken a mind to put down roots. My mind is like that, wandering all over the place, alighting here and there with no particular purpose. It thinks it knows what it's doing, but a butterfly has more focused direction. So I sit. What I do with my mind isn't important and probably wouldn't work for anyone else. I sit. I breathe. And at some point, that surely must be magic because my own poor will has nothing to do with it, a little bubble—not of mental chatter but of deep stillness—forms inside me. Now I can begin to listen. I don't have roots yet, just little thread-like rootlets, but they're enough to keep me in one place long enough for that bubble to do its work.

Some days—heck, who am I kidding? most days—my writing begins with a similar process. I can find almost any excuse not to sit down in front of the computer or with pad and pen in hand. It's not that I don't want to write or I'm not excited about the story I'm working on. I know intellectually that once I'm into the flow, I'll lose myself in it. I love my characters and miss them, even overnight. But some part of my brain, my monkey-chattering, time-frivoling, recalcitrant part of my brain, runs amok.

I can get into a death match with that monkey-mind, grimly insisting that we will sit down. No. Matter. What. Sometimes I need that 5th turbo-charged gear. I have deadlines, I get caught with too many projects and one of life's inevitable sand-in-the-gears crises. Then I need to be able to put Ms. Idiot-Monkey on ice and plunge into work-on-steroids mode.

Most of the time, however, my schedule is a bit less frantic. On some days, I'm ready to go as soon as I've finished breakfast, or even before. Yet on other days, I don't "settle" until an hour or two before dinner. I go through much the same process as I do at Quaker meeting. I wait. I listen. I try to pay attention to what I need in order to be ready to write. The very concept of being *ready* to write took me years to formulate. Partly because I have insanely high expectations of myself and partly because I began writing professionally when my children were small and there was no such thing as transition or warm-up time, I think I should be prepared to write at any moment. The truth is that when I do that, I have to rip out a lot of what I produce. If, on the other hand, I am able to pay attention to what my creative mind needs, I am much more likely to work well and productively.

After some years of trying to listen to myself, I realized that most of the time, the things standing in my way were not frivolous or unrelated to my writing. As often as not, I discovered a niggling plot problem, a lapse in tone, or a character aching to point me in a better direction in yesterday's work. Or a new story idea that will quite happily go back to sleep once I've jotted it down. Or something in my life that is moving beneath the story, awkwardly and silently, waiting for my attention to bring it to life.

Listen. Pay attention. Settle. Put down roots deep into your story, deep into your life.

Notes

About the Author

Deborah J. Ross is an award-nominated writer and editor of fantasy and science fiction, with over a dozen traditionally published novels and five dozen short stories in print. Recent releases include *Thunderlord* and *The Children of Kings* (with Marion Zimmer Bradley), *Collaborators* (Lambda Literary Finalist, as Deborah Wheeler), and The Seven-Petaled Shield trilogy. Her short fiction has appeared in The Magazine of Science Fiction and Fantasy, Asimov's, Star Wars: Tales from Jabba's Palace, and the Book View Café anthology *Nevertheless She Persisted*, and has earned honorable mention in Year's Best SF. She has served as Secretary to the Science Fiction and Fantasy Writers of America (SFWA), is a member of Book View Café, and chaired the jury for the Philip K. Dick Award. When she's not writing, she knits for charity, plays classical piano, and studies yoga.

Also by Deborah J. Ross

Darkover novels (with Marion Zimmer Bradley)
The Laran Gambit (forthcoming)
Thunderlord
The Children of Kings
Hastur Lord
The Alton Gift
A Flame in Hali
Zandru's Forge
The Fall of Neskaya

The Seven-Petaled Shield trilogy
The Heir of Khored
Shannivar
The Seven-Petaled Shield

Collaborators* (forthcoming)
Northlight*
Jaydium*

Collections
Transfusion and Other Tales of Hope*
Azkhantian Tales*
Other Doorways: Early Novels*
Pearls of Fire, Dreams of Steel*

*available in BVC editions

About Book View Café

Book View Café Publishing Cooperative is an author-owned cooperative of over fifty professional writers, publishing in a variety of genres such as fantasy, romance, mystery, and science fiction.

BVC authors include *New York Times* and *USA Today* bestsellers; Nebula, Hugo, and Philip K. Dick Award winners; World Fantasy Award, Campbell Award, and RITA Award nominees; and winners and nominees of many other publishing awards.

Since its debut in 2008, BVC has gained a reputation for producing high-quality e-books, and is now bringing that same quality to its print editions.

www.ingramcontent.com/pod-product-compliance
Lightning Source LLC
Chambersburg PA
CBHW060520080526
44586CB00012B/551